Chuck and Blanche Johnso

# Savor Idaho Cookbook

## *Idaho's Finest Restaurants & Lodges Their Recipes & Their Histories*

Wilderness Adventures Press, Inc.™
Belgrade, Montana

Published by Wilderness Adventures Press, Inc.™
45 Buckskin Road
Belgrade, MT 59714
1-866-400-2012
Web site: www.wildadvpress.com
E-mail: books@wildadvpress.com
First Edition



Printed in Singapore

ISBN 1-932098-21-6

Other Titles Available In This Series

Savor Denver
Savor Montana
Savor Montana II
Savor Oregon
Savor Portland
Savor Seattle
Savor Wildgame

# Table of Contents

## – Ketchum –



## – Hailey –

## – Pocatello –

*Women trout fishing in Boise River. Ca. 1920*

*Wanigans (rafts) at the mouth of Beaver Creek. 125 miles up river from Lewiston on the north fork of the Clearwater. They served as bunk house and cook shack for crew that drove 35 to 50 million feet of logs from the Clearwater forest to the mill pond at Lewiston. Wanigans are 80 feet long, made of cedar logs and bound together with wild cherry vines.*

# INTRODUCTION

Idaho is a richly varied state in many ways. Geographically, the state contains pine-covered mountains and pristine lakes and streams, as well as sagebrush-covered desert, spectacular lava formations, and rich soils for growing wonderful produce. Economically, Idaho plays host to several large international corporations, supports a growing wine industry, and produces much of the food consumed in the state as well as exporting it to states throughout the West. As a recreational destination, Idaho is growing in popularity throughout the country.

Thus, it is no wonder that the restaurants of Idaho and their chefs are beginning to be noticed nationally. The intermountain region has become much more conscious of the explosion of flavor when fresh and local ingredients are used in culinary presentations. Many of the chefs featured in this book follow this philosophy, and have a great selection of local produce and meats at their fingertips. The reader can also take advantage of this selection. Check out the Culinary Sources listed in the back of this book for farms and ranches in and around Idaho.

It is important to note that all of the featured restaurants were by invitation. None of the restaurants were charged for appearing in this book. We selected them based on the excellence and uniqueness of their food, as well as their ambience. Many have interesting histories. We also looked for places that feature comprehensive wine lists. We want to thank the owners, managers, chefs, and all the restaurant staff members who participated in getting this project to fruition.

We also want to thank the staff at the Idaho State Historical Society in Boise and the Appaloosa Museum & Heritage Center in Moscow for their help in obtaining historical photographs that you will see throughout this cookbook. We also want to thank or friends, Gary and Martha Bauer of Hope, Idaho for their recommendations of restaurants in northern Idaho.

The reader can use this book in several ways. As a travel guide, the reader can learn something about a restaurant's history, philosophy, and ambience, as well as the type of cuisine that it features. The map in the front gives the reader a perspective of the state and approximately where each restaurant is located.

Reading the recipes is a fun way to get a "taste" of each restaurant, and trying them out at home can be fun for the home chef as well as his or her guests.

Blanche and Chuck Johnson

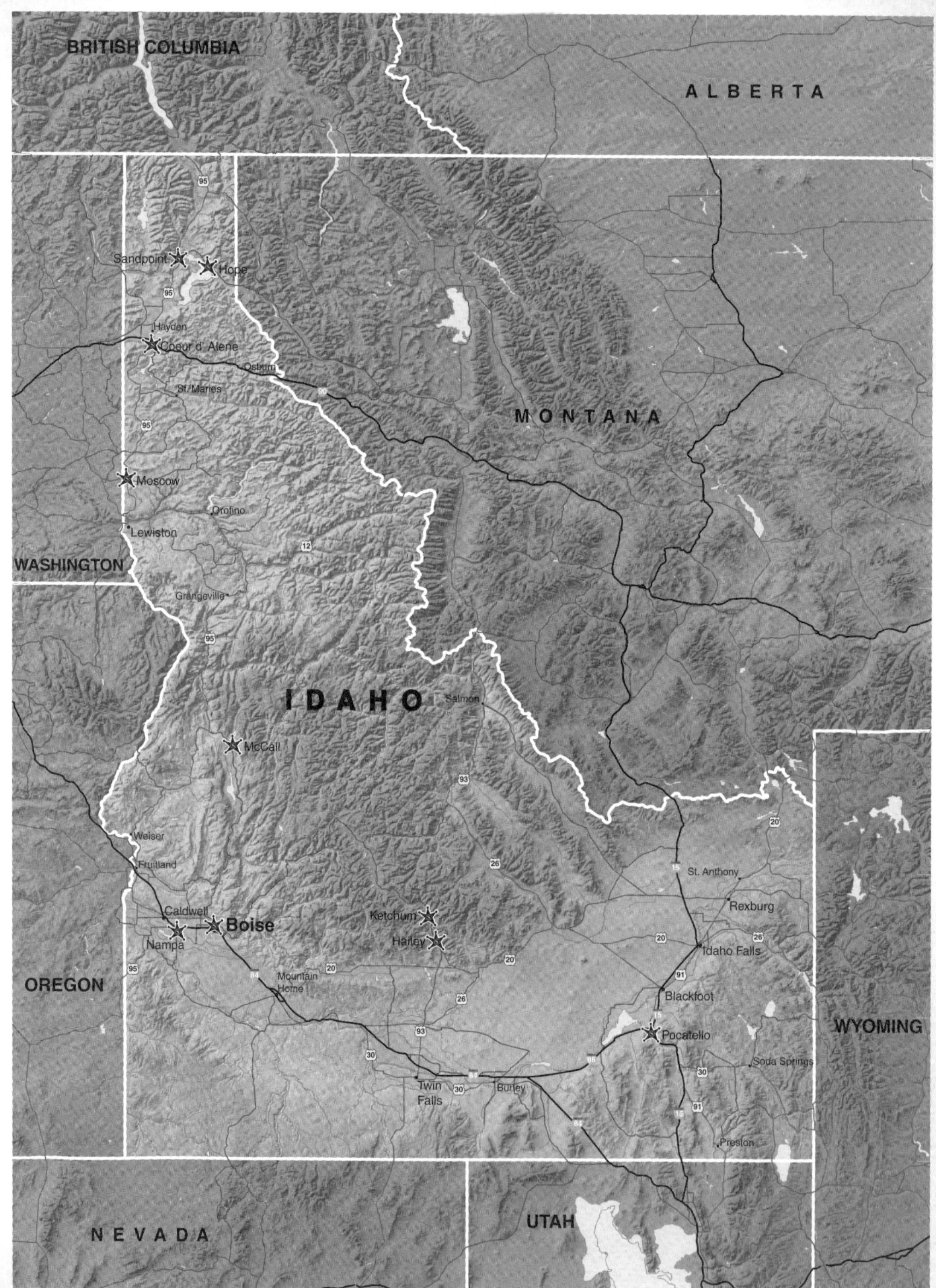
BRITISH COLUMBIA
ALBERTA
MONTANA
WASHINGTON
IDAHO
OREGON
WYOMING
NEVADA
UTAH
Sandpoint
Hope
Hayden
Coeur d' Alene
Osburn
St. Maries
Moscow
Orofino
Lewiston
Grangeville
Salmon
McCall
Weiser
Fruitland
Caldwell
Boise
Nampa
Ketchum
Hailey
Mountain Home
St. Anthony
Rexburg
Idaho Falls
Blackfoot
Pocatello
Soda Springs
Twin Falls
Burley
Preston

# Savor Idaho Cookbook

## Restaurants Featured

Sandpoint
- Ivano's Ristorante
- The Lodge at Hidden Lakes
- Sand Creek Grill

Hope
- Beyond Hope

Couer d'Alene
- Bonsai Bistro
- Brix
- The Wine Cellar

Moscow
- Red Door

McCall
- Epicurean

Nampa
- Copper Canyon

Boise
- Andrea's
- Angell's Bar and Grill
- Asiago's
- Bar Gernika
- Cottonwood Grill
- Emilio's
- The Game Keeper Restaurant
- Le Café de Paris
- The Milky Way
- Mortimers

Ketchum
- Chandler's Restaurant
- Felix's Restaurant
- Ketchum Grill
- The Roosevelt Tavern and Grill
- The Sawtooth Club

Hailey
- CK's

Pocatello
- The Continental Bistro
- Remo's

**Restaurant Locations**

0 100 Miles

0 100 KM

# Idaho Facts

**Admission to Statehood:**
July 3, 1890
**Fourteenth largest state in the union**
83,557 square miles
305 miles east to west
479 miles north to south
**Elevations** - 770 feet to 12,662 feet
**Counties** - 44
**Population (2005)** - 1,429,096

*Picnic at Rock Creek in Gem County with people from Pearl, Idaho. ca. 1907*

4 Indian Reservations
9 National Parks
13 National Forests
7 Wilderness Areas
27 State Parks
2 National Monuments
1 National Reserve
**Nickname**:
Gem State

**Primary Industries**
Agriculture
Lumber
Mining
Tourism
**Capital** - Boise
**Bird** - Mountain Bluebird
**Animal** - Appalooza
**Flower** - Syringa
**Fish** - Cutthroat trout
**Tree** - Western White Pine
**Gemstone** - Idaho Star Garnet

*Chief Joseph*

# Ivano's Ristorante

102 S. 1st Avenue #101
Sandpoint, ID 83864
208-263-0211
www.ivanossandpoint.com

Dinner daily from 5:00pm
Ivano's Caffè open Monday – Friday
7:00am to 4:00pm

# Ivano's Ristorante

### *Jim Lippi and Rich Ballard, Owners*

On the corner of First and Pine sits a three-story building, which houses Ivano's Ristorante and Caffè. The building is set back from the corner, allowing the restaurant to have a large patio space for dining on the many spectacular summer nights that are experienced in Sandpoint, Idaho. The first floor of the building comprises both the Ristorante and the Caffè. While the Ristorante serves dinner, the Caffè is open weekdays, and features fresh pastries, gourmet organic fair-trade Kicking Horse Coffee and fresh made luncheon specials.

Ivano's Ristorante has the grand distinction of being the oldest owner-operated restaurant in the area, being in business for over 23 years. Ivano's started as a way for Jim Lippi to move his family to Sandpoint and has become a labor of love. The restaurant was named as a tribute to Jim's father, Ivano Lippi who immigrated to the United States in 1938. Settling in California, Ivano chose to live his life as a restaurateur, using hard work and imagination to create a comfortable life for his family and himself. However, his journey ended before his dream was complete. Jim opened Ivano's Ristorante in February 1984, regarding it as the completion of his father's dream. The restaurant was originally in a small house at the corner of 2nd and Lake before moving to its current location.

Dining at Ivano's is a pleasurable experience, reminiscent of a friendly restaurant in Tuscany. When entering, you will notice a large wine display behind the bar with selections from Italy and California, as well as many award winning Northwest wines. The local wine maker at Pend Oreille Winery, Jim Gardetto, makes a special house wine exclusively for Ivano's: Jimmy Gardetto Vino Rosso. The wine is named after his grandfather, who used to make his own wine. The dedicated wait staff, with most employed for over six years, will cater to your needs.

The soft yellow walls of the dining room give a warm and cheery note to a restaurant that is a favorite among the locals. Large floor-to-ceiling glass doors overlook the patio, which is lit with tiny Italian lights and decorated with large containers overflowing with brilliant flowers. The extensive menu of true northern Italian specialties will tempt any diner: wonderful dishes of veal, chicken, and fresh fish, along with mouth-watering steaks and locally raised buffalo, abundant pasta dishes, soups, salads, and antipasti. It's not surprising that *Ski Magazine* voted Ivano's *Best Restaurant in the Pacific Northwest* and the *Spokesman Review* awarded it *Best Dining in Sandpoint* in 1997.

# Parmesan Crusted Halibut

Fish and cheese are not a traditional Italian pairing. However, the thin layer of Parmesan adds a nice texture as well as another element of flavor, to balance the mild flavor of the halibut.

## Ingredients

- *2 6-ounce halibut filets*
- *⅓ cup olive oil*
- *2 eggs*
- *½ cup Parmesan cheese, shredded*
- *¼ cup flour*
- *2 tablespoons butter*
- *1 teaspoon lemon juice*
- *2 drops Tabasco sauce*
- *½ cup white wine*
- *kosher salt and black pepper to taste*
- *fresh parsley, chopped for garnish*

## Preparation

HEAT oven to 350 degrees. Place a non-stick sauté pan on medium heat with olive oil Allow oil to become hot. In a bowl, mix eggs and Parmesan cheese. Season halibut with salt and pepper and dredge in flour. Dip one side into egg and cheese mixture and carefully place in hot oil with the egg and cheese side down. When nicely browned, turn over and put in 350-degree oven for 8 minutes.

REMOVE from oven, and remove fish from pan. Pour off all oil. Add butter, a pinch of the dredging flour, lemon juice, Tabasco sauce, and wine and stir to combine. Reduce until a slightly thickened consistency is achieved. If it is too thick, add a little more wine; if too thin, add more butter. Keep pan moving and do not allow sauce to become too hot, as it will break down. Pour over fish and garnish with fresh parsley.

***Serves 2***

*Wine suggestions: Pinot Grigio or Chardonnay*

# Pesce con Herbe Fresco

*(Fish with Fresh Herbs)*

This is a very common Tuscan marinade. It can be used on a variety of charbroiled items, from meats to vegetables. I think it is especially good on fish. You will need a blender and good quality fresh herbs and olive oil. The marinade resembles a pesto, but has a more fluid consistency.

## Ingredients

*2 ounces rosemary*
*2 ounces sage*
*2 ounces thyme*
*4 ounces parsley*
*4 ounces basil*
*¼ cup garlic cloves*
*4 drops Tabasco sauce*
*2 tablespoons lemon juice*
*¼ cup white wine*
*2 cups olive oil*
*kosher salt and black pepper to taste*
*2 6- to 8-ounce fish filets. mahi-mahi, tuna, or other firm-fleshed fish*
*2 tablespoons butter*
*1 lemon, sliced*

## Preparation

PLACE herbs, garlic, Tabasco, lemon juice, and white wine in blender, and pulse to grind up herbs and garlic. Slowly add olive oil to emulsify. Season to taste with salt and pepper. Place fish in a shallow pan. Pour enough marinade over fish to just cover one side. Turn over and repeat. Allow to stand for about 20 minutes.

PREPARE char broiler. When hot, rub with some oil to help prevent sticking. Grill must be clean. Grill fish to desired doneness, basting with some of the marinade. Remove to a platter and keep warm. In a sauté pan, put butter and ¼ cup of the marinade. Heat just enough to melt the butter and warm the mixture. Pour over fish. Any extra marinade will stay a week in the refrigerator. Serve fish with sliced lemon.

***Serves 2***

*Wine suggestions: Pinot Grigio or Chenin Blanc*

# Anatra di Padella

*(Duck in the Pan)*

A very savory and satisfying preparation that is representative of the cuisine of Bologna. The original recipe has been altered by substituting dried cranberry for sun-dried tomato. We made the change for a Christmas event, thinking it would add to the festivity. The response was very positive, so we kept the change.

## Ingredients

- *2 duck breasts, domestic or wild, skin on*
- *2 ounces extra virgin olive oil*
- *1 tablespoon butter*
- *2 shallots, chopped*
- *6 fresh sage leaves*
- *1 teaspoon black peppercorns, cracked*
- *4 ounces fortified stock*
- *1 ounce brandy*
- *2 ounces heavy cream*
- *3 ounces dried cranberries*

## Preparation

HEAT oven to 350 degrees. Season duck breasts on each side with salt and pepper. Place breasts in a medium-hot pan with olive oil, starting with skin side down. When well browned on both sides, place in 350-degree oven for 7 or 8 minutes.

POUR off all but about one-third of the oil in the pan and add butter, shallots, sage, and peppercorns. When shallots are a light brown in color and sage leaves are crispy, add stock, brandy, cream, and cranberries. Reduce until sauce moves around together. Remove duck from oven and allow to rest. Slice breasts against the grain, arrange on plate, and pour sauce over.

***Serves 2***

*Wine suggestion: a full-bodied red, such as a Zinfandel*

*Stagecoach crossing Continental Divide in Salmon River Country.*

# *The Lodge at Hidden Lakes*

151 Clubhouse Way
Sandpoint, ID 83864
208-263-1642
888-80-MOOSE (806-6673)
www.hiddenlakesgolf.com

Daily for lunch and dinner
Sunday brunch

# The Lodge at Hidden Lakes

### *Paul Donaghue, Executive Chef*

A leisurely drive anywhere around the Sandpoint area is a true delight, with the pine-scented mountain air and the sparkling waters of Lake Pend Oreille. But the drive to Hidden Lakes is special as you reach your destination at the clubhouse. Located eight miles from Sandpoint on Scenic Byway 200 at milepost 28, turn north onto Clubhouse Way and drive past some of the lush fairways of the challenging golf course before you arrive at the clubhouse.

This 17,000 square foot massive log structure holds the golf shop and member club rooms as well as the public lounge and restaurant. Walk through the entryway into an interior of walls made of massive polished white pine, with floor-to-ceiling glass windows overlooking the putting green and the Pack River. Anchoring each end of this huge space are two and a half story rock fireplaces. In the center is a natural cedar trunk, six feet in diameter, estimated to be about 400 years old. The developer rescued it intact, as it was being taken to the sawmill. Gaze upward and you will see a life-size moose head carved out of one of its limbs. The antlers were carved out of the remainder of the tree after it was topped off to fit inside the vaulted ceiling.

The restaurant is cozy on cool evenings with the fire in the immense rock fireplace. The upholstered white pine chairs add to the casually elegant surroundings, and the room is softly lit from the moose antler chandeliers. When the weather permits, dining on the 20-foot wide deck that overlooks the Pack River is a special experience. Enjoy the occasional flight of Canadian geese and at dusk, you might even see a moose stroll down to the river.

The restaurant was opened in June 2001, under the expert eye of Executive Chef Paul Donaghue. Before opening the restaurant, Chef Paul had spent many years living and working throughout the West. His previous position was with Café Rosemary in Bend, Oregon. Chef Paul enjoys cooking with fresh local ingredients, when available, such as locally raised lamb and fresh morels from the surrounding mountains. He also specializes in tantalizing dishes of wild game, and knows how to pair the perfect wine with each dish. The restaurant is a consistent winner of the Award of Excellence from Wine Spectator magazine, as well as winning the National Restaurant Association's Award of Excellence. This is a special place for a romantic and relaxing evening.

# Summer Tomato Relish

This relish is perfect with any grilled fish, or as an antipasto when tossed together with fresh buffalo mozzarella. It also works as a perfect garnish for the Dungeness Crab Cakes. If you have yellow and red tomatoes this makes a wonderfully colorful dish.

## Ingredients

- *1 pint grape or cherry tomatoes, quartered*
- *5 ounces red onion, diced*
- *1 tablespoon garlic, minced*
- *¼ cup firmly packed fresh basil, chopped*
- *1 teaspoon cilantro, minced*
- *½ teaspoon cayenne pepper*
- *1 teaspoon sugar*
- *2 limes*
- *2 lemons*
- *¼ cup olive oil*
- *salt and pepper to taste*

ZEST the lemons and limes and then juice them, discarding the rinds. Combine the zest and juices with all other ingredients in a large non-reactive bowl. Toss well to combine. This relish will last up to 3 days if put into an airtight container.

***Yield: 3 cups***

*Wine suggestion: a crisp Sauvignon Blanc*

# Dungeness Crab Cakes

## Ingredients

- 1 *tablespoon butter*
- 7 *scallions, minced*
- 7 *ounces scallops, abductor removed and excess moisture pressed out*
- 1 *egg*
- 1 *cup heavy cream*
- 1 *tablespoon Dijon mustard*
- 1 *teaspoon Tabasco sauce*
- ½ *teaspoon Worcestershire sauce*
- ½ *pound lump Dungeness crabmeat, excess moisture pressed out*
- *salt and pepper to taste*
- *Summer Tomato Relish for garnish (see recipe in this section)*

## Preparation

HEAT butter in a sauté pan on low heat. When hot, add scallions and sweat for 3 minutes or until just soft. Remove from heat and let cool.

PLACE scallops into a work bowl of a food processor. Pulse until scallop meat is blended well. While processor is running, add egg and process 30 seconds. Stop machine and use rubber spatula to scrape down the sides of the bowl. Start machine up again and slowly add cream, mustard, Tabasco and Worcestershire. Mix well until blended and smooth. Remove mixture and place in a large mixing bowl. Add crabmeat and scallion mixture and blend well. Adjust seasonings with salt and pepper.

HEAT oven to 450 degrees. Using a large sauté pan, add a small amount of oil and put over high heat. Measure out ¼ cup of crab mixture at a time, form into a cake, and put in sauté pan. Brown cakes for 45 seconds on each side and place in 450-degree oven for 3-4 minutes. Garnish with Summer Tomato Relish.

***Serves 8 as an appetizer***

*Wine suggestion: an "unoaked" Chardonnay*

# Crème Brulée

You will need a small propane torch to finish this dessert. You can find the torches at any hardware store.

## Ingredients

- 10 *egg yolks*
- 1¾ *cups heavy cream*
- 3½ *cups whole milk*
- 1 *vanilla bean, split and seeds scraped out*
- 2 *cinnamon sticks*
- ¾ *cup sugar*
- *extra sugar for finishing*

## Preparation

HEAT oven to 300 degrees. Beat egg yolks until smooth and set aside. Put cream and milk into a large saucepan with vanilla bean, cinnamon sticks, and sugar. On low heat, bring mixture to a simmer and continue simmering for 35 minutes. Remove from heat and let cinnamon and vanilla bean steep for another 25 minutes. Remove cinnamon sticks and vanilla bean and SLOWLY pour cream and milk mixture into the beaten eggs, beating slowly while pouring.

POUR mixture into 8-ounce porcelain ramekins. Place ramekins in a large baking dish deep enough to hold them. After ramekins are in baking pan, pour enough water into pan to come three-quarters of the way up the sides of the ramekins. Place pan in 300-degree oven and cover with another baking dish of the same size. Bake for 45 minutes, or until brulées are set. Slightly loose is fine. Remove from oven and let sit until the water is cool. Place in refrigerator to chill completely.

WHEN ready to serve, sprinkle very lightly with sugar and caramelize the top of each brulée with a small propane torch. When golden brown and surface is hard to touch, they are ready to serve.

***Serves 10***

*Wine suggestion: a dessert wine such as a late harvest Semillon*

*Challenging green at Hidden Lakes Golf Course.*

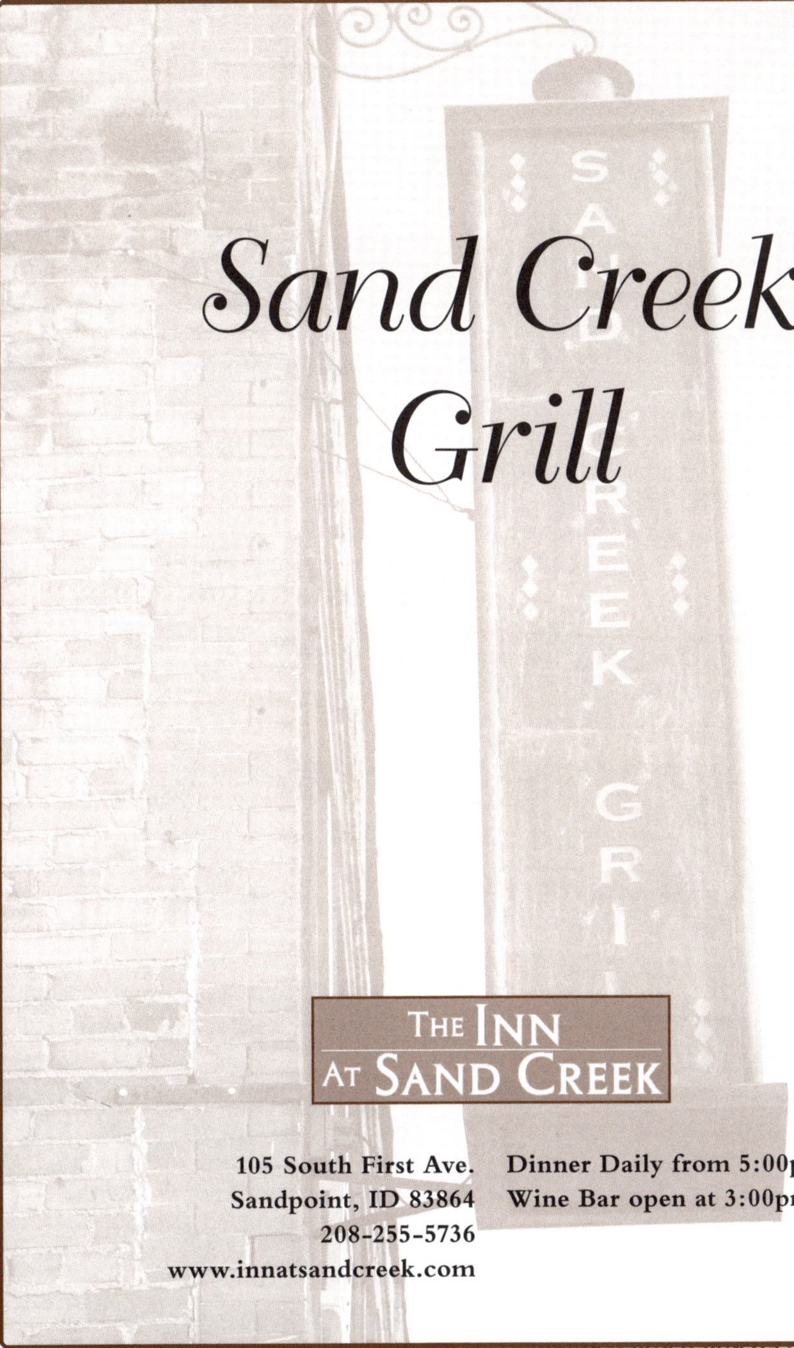

# *Sand Creek Grill*

THE INN AT SAND CREEK

105 South First Ave.
Sandpoint, ID 83864
208-255-5736
www.innatsandcreek.com

Dinner Daily from 5:00pm
Wine Bar open at 3:00pm

# Sand Creek Grill

### *Gloria and Jennings Waterhouse, Owners*

A lovely old building in downtown Sandpoint has been turned into a wonderful retreat. Gloria Waterhouse and her daughter, Jennings, have created a comfortable upscale inn and restaurant out of what was once the Fidelity Trust Bank Building. Built in 1909, the brick building was one of the first permanent buildings erected in this part of town, when Sandpoint was a new and bustling log town.

Raised in the South, Gloria has the southern tradition of entertaining people and making them feel welcome. She and Jennings love to rehabilitate old structures. Their love of historic design was the inspiration for preserving this beautiful old building. Old brick walls surround the bar and dining area and the flooring is worn, wide plank pine boards. Even the original bank vaults remain and are in use for wine storage and refrigeration. The main dining areas boast 16-foot ceilings, but give a warm feel with the use of a rich Asian red lacquered finish on the walls and multiple candle-lit sconces, as well as an abundance of aged copper trim banking the bar and the windows. The rear of the restaurant opens onto Sand Creek and the marina, facing Lake Pend Oreille and the Green Monarch Mountains. This is a lovely setting for dining on a beautiful summer's evening.

After planning the lush three-suite inn, Chef Ian Wingate of Spokane approached Gloria about opening a fine dining establishment in the inn and suggested a menu featuring a French-Asian theme. Shortly after opening the grill, Chef Wingate was awarded the position of Executive Chef for the newly renovated Davenport Hotel, but his influence is still seen in the lovely dishes served at the grill today. The menu celebrates the changing seasons and the local bounty, representing a fusion of Northwest cuisine with notable Asian influences. Sushi Thursdays have become a popular tradition at the grill as well. Start off you meal with a homemade soup of the day served with freshly baked bread, or one of the delightful salads, followed by a traditional entrée, or try several of the Small Plate selections to share with your companions.

Wine lovers will enjoy the many wines offered by the glass, as well as an extensive list of wines by the bottle. There is a large selection of Northwest and California wines, as well an abundant offering from France, Italy, South Africa, Germany, Australia, Argentina, Chile, and Spain. A large selection of tap and bottle beers, including imported as well as unique American brews are also offered.

# Roasted Winter Squash and Fennel Soup

## Ingredients

- 2 *butternut squash, peeled and seeded*
- 2 *acorn squash, peeled and seeded*
- 3 *fennel bulbs, rough chopped*
- *salt and pepper*
- 1 *yellow onion, fine dice*
- *olive oil*
- 1 *cup roasted garlic*
- 1 *cup fresh horseradish, grated*
- ⅛ *cup cumin*
- ⅛ *cup coriander*
- ⅛ *cup yellow curry*
- 2 *quarts chicken stock*
- 2 *quarts heavy cream*
- 1 *pint half & half*

## Prepartion

HEAT oven to 375 degrees. Season squash with salt and pepper, and roast in oven with fennel until soft. In a stockpot, sauté onion in a little olive oil until translucent, about 5 minutes. Add squash, fennel, garlic, horseradish, and spices. Sauté for 5 more minutes. Add chicken stock and bring to a boil. Blend soup in food processor until smooth. Return to pot and bring back to a slow simmer. Finish by adding cream and half & half and bring back to a simmer. Serve immediately.

***Serves 10***

# PEAR SALAD

*with Caramelized Walnuts, Gorgonzola, and Apple Cider Vinaigrette*

## Ingredients

- *4 cups spring mix greens*
- *Apple Cider Vinaigrette (recipe follows)*
- *2 ripe pears*
- *½ cup Gorgonzola, crumbled*
- *Caramelized Walnuts (recipe follows)*

## Preparation

DICE 1 pear and add it to spring mix, tossing with some of the Apple Cider Vinaigrette. Stack on a plate. Sprinkle with Gorgonzola and Caramelized Walnuts. Thinly slice remaining pear and fan to garnish salad.

***Serves 2***

## For the Apple Cider Vinaigrette

- *2 pears, peeled and cored*
- *½ cup sugar*
- *1 cup apple cider vinegar*
- *1 tablespoon olive oil*

IN FOOD processor or blender, purée pears and sugar. Add apple cider vinegar and blend until smooth. Slowly add olive oil and blend until well combined. The dressing should be very tart.

## For the Caramelized Walnuts

- *walnuts*
- *honey*
- *brown sugar*

IN A large pan, combine walnuts, honey, brown sugar, and a splash of water. Place over low heat and continue to stir mixture, making sure walnuts don't burn. Cook until gooey and well caramelized. Remove from heat and separate walnuts onto a sheet pan covered with wax paper. Let cool. Do not cover or refrigerate.

# Roasted Garlic Crusted Ahi

*with Wasabi Plum Sauce*

## Ingredients

*4 6-ounce Ahi steaks – Sushi grade, about ½-inch thick*
*2 heads garlic*
*olive oil*
*salt and pepper to taste*
*Wasabi Plum Sauce (recipe follows)*

## Preparation

HEAT oven to 400 degrees. Drizzle a little olive oil over the garlic heads and roast them in the oven until they are soft. Remove cloves from skins and smash to make a past. Chill garlic, and then season with salt and pepper. Rub each side of the tuna steaks with the garlic to make a crust.

SEAR the crusted tuna in a very hot pan for about 20 seconds on each side. Tuna should be rare. Serve with a large dollop of Wasabi Plum Sauce on top.

***Serves 4***

*Wine suggestion: Elk Cove Pinot Noir, Willamette Valley, Oregon*

## For the Wasabi Plum Sauce

*⅛ cup wasabi powder*
*2½ cups heavy cream*
*2 plums, blanched, skinned, pitted, and puréed*

COMBINE wasabi powder and cream in a food processor and blend until stiff peaks have formed. Fold in the plum purée.

# Cedar Planked Wild King Salmon

*with Sweet Chili Béarnaise & Marinated Artichoke Salad*

## Ingredients

- 4 *8-ounce wild king salmon steaks*
- ¾ *teaspoon ground turmeric*
- ¾ *teaspoon ground cardamom*
- ¾ *teaspoon ground coriander*
- ¾ *teaspoon granulated garlic*
- ¾ *teaspoon paprika*
- 1 *tablespoon fresh thyme, minced*
- *Sweet Chili Béarnaise (recipe follows)*
- *Marinated Artichoke Salad (recipe follows)*

## Preparation

SOAK an untreated cedar plank in water for at least 4 hours. Heat oven to 350 degrees. Heat soaked plank in oven for 30 minutes.

COMBINE the spices and rub salmon steaks generously with the mixture. Place steaks on heated and soaked cedar plank. Place in 350-degree oven and bake for about 10 minutes. We like to serve ours medium rare, so they don't dry out.

SERVE immediately with Sweet Chili Béarnaise and Marinated Artichoke Salad.

***Serves 4***

*Wine suggestion: L'Ecole No. 41 Barrel Fermented Semillon, Columbia Valley, Washington*

## For the Sweet Chili Béarnaise

- 6 *egg yolks*
- *juice of ½ lemon*
- 2 *teaspoons Tabasco sauce*
- 2 *tablespoons Thai sweet chili sauce (Mae Ploy)*
- ¼ *cup red wine*
- ⅓ *cup fresh tarragon, chopped*
- 2½ - 3 *cups melted butter*

COMBINE egg yolks, lemon juice, Tabasco, and Thai chili sauce in a bowl. In a sauté pan, combine red wine and tarragon. Bring to a simmer on medium-low heat until Au Sec, almost all the wine is evaporated. Set aside. Over double boiler on low, whisk melted butter into egg mixture until desired consistency if achieved. Be careful not to break the sauce. Remove from heat and add tarragon reduction. Keep at room temperature while salmon is cooking.

## For the Marinated Artichoke Salad

- *4 cups lightly packed marinated artichoke hearts*
- *⅔ cup feta cheese, crumbled*
- *⅔ cup buffalo mozzarella, diced*
- *⅓ cup fresh basil chiffonade*
- *2 cups grape tomatoes, halved*
- *⅛ cup olive oil*
- *⅛ cup balsamic vinegar*
- *salt and pepper to taste*

COMBINE all ingredients, toss lightly, and serve.

# Mesquite Smoked Buffalo Short Ribs

We often serve this comfort food on cold winter days over steamed jasmine rice or creamy polenta.

## Ingredients

- *5 pounds buffalo short ribs*
- *1 large onion, chopped*
- *4 celery stalks, chopped*
- *1 carrot, chopped*
- *10 garlic cloves, finely chopped*
- *3 large sprigs fresh rosemary, chopped*
- *5 cups Cabernet Sauvignon*
- *6 cups beef stock*
- *1 cup Hoisin*
- *1 cup water*
- *⅓ cup fresh horseradish, grated*
- *½ cup soy sauce*
- *3 cups pineapple juice*
- *cornstarch slurry (1 cup cornstarch mixed with 1½ cups cold water)*

## Preparation

PLACE short ribs on a sheet pan and smoke them over mesquite for about 4 hours at 160 degrees. Save the drippings.

IN A large braising pan, sauté onion, celery, and carrot about 5-7 minutes. Add garlic and rosemary and sauté for 3 more minutes. Add rest of ingredients, except the cornstarch slurry and bring to a simmer. Add smoked short ribs and their drippings and cook for about 45 minutes, or until rib meat is tender.

REMOVE ribs. Add cornstarch slurry to thicken liquid. Bring back to boil for 5 minutes. Strain liquid and serve over ribs.

***Serves 10***

*Wine suggestion: Nelms Road Cabernet Sauvignon, Columbia Valley, Washington*

# *Beyond Hope*

# Beyond Hope

***Jim Lane, Proprietor***
***Bill Hibish, Chef***
***Cathy Dela'o, Food & Beverage Manager***

If you happen to be in the vicinity of beautiful Lake Pend Oreille anytime between May and September, treat yourself to a unique dining experience at Beyond Hope Resort. Imagine relaxing on the spacious wood deck with your favorite beverage and watching the spectacular sunset over the lake and the Cabinet Mountains. Located in the midst of a wildlife preserve, the resort offers a chance to observe whitetail deer browsing throughout the grounds. The resort seems to foster a feeling of camaraderie among its guests. Even a first-time stranger will feel completely at home here and want to return year after year.

In 1968, Spokane real estate broker, Bob Jones, purchased the land on the Hope Peninsula, bringing his family to enjoy the Idaho summers. In 1974 the family constructed the building that is now the restaurant and bar, and in 1975 the RV Park was opened. The resort became a very popular family destination, with travelers coming from all over the country and from Canada. Every season Bob and his family would prepare their famous "Hobo Dinner". Guests would bring their own utensils for a feast of local sausage, potatoes, and vegetables cooked in gleaming galvanized garbage pails over hot coals. The family had created a spot that would be memorable for many other families.

After Bob's passing in 1986, the family continued to run the resort until 1997, when they reluctantly voted to sell the resort. In 1998, Jim Lane purchased the property. With the help of his partner, Cathy Dela'o and their daughter, Gena, Jim renewed Bob's special touch to the resort: repairing the property and adding a kitchen to fulfill his dream of creating a fine dining establishment. As the new owners spent more time at the resort, and as they began to manage it themselves, they grew to love it as Bob Jones and his family had. This special feeling shows through in the care they take of their customers and guests, many of whom return each year as to a big family reunion.

Presiding over the kitchen is Chef Bill Hibish, an Idaho native who began his culinary career at the Hyatt Regency Kaanapali in Maui, Hawaii. He later worked at several well-known restaurants in the Greater Seattle area. Although he enjoyed his time at world-class resorts and big city restaurants, Chef Bill dreamt of running a small restaurant where he would be able to control all aspects of his culinary work. Beyond Hope fit the bill, and you will enjoy the succulent and sophisticated dishes that he prepares for you to enjoy in this spectacular, rustic setting.

# Wild Mushroom Risotto

We like to use local morels that we dry in the spring. This recipe is wonderful as a side dish with beef, lamb, or pork. It is also a nice complement to salmon, swordfish, or marlin. Chef's tip: Risotto is a time-sensitive item that needs to be served immediately as it can overcook and become gummy. You can avoid this by preparing the recipe a few hours (or a day) before serving. Stop the preparation before you add the mushrooms, cheese, and cream. Spread the risotto on a cookie sheet and refrigerate. About 20 minutes before serving, reheat the rice and finish the recipe.

## Ingredients

*2 tablespoons fresh shallots, minced*
*2 tablespoons fresh garlic, minced*
*4 tablespoons clarified butter*
*1 cup white wine*
*2 cups Arborio rice*
*2 ounces morel mushrooms, hydrated in 5 cups hot water mixed with 2 tablespoons mushroom base*
*1⅕ cups heavy cream*
*2 ounces Fontina cheese*
*4 ounces crimini mushrooms, sliced*

## Preparation

SAUTÉ shallots and garlic in butter until translucent, but not browned. Deglaze pan with the white wine and reduce by half. Add rice, stirring constantly until liquid is absorbed. Remove morels from hot water and add water, ¼ cup at a time, to rice. Be sure that at the end of this process, you do not pour the dirt from the bottom of the container into the rice. Utilize all liquid, stirring constantly.

ADD cream, stirring constantly, until ¾ absorbed. Add cheese and mushrooms, stirring constantly, until cheese melts.

SERVE immediately.

***Serves 6***

# Truffled Rice Cakes

Our kitchen is small and we don't have a lot of space to hold hot side dishes. We don't serve baked potatoes, and we wanted some interesting alternatives to mashed potatoes or plain rice.

## Ingredients

- *1½ cups Calrose rice*
- *3 cups water*
- *3 ounces goat cheese*
- *2 tablespoons truffle oil*

## Preparation

COOK rice in water. While rice is still warm, add goat cheese and truffle oil, mixing well. Spread evenly, one inch thick, on half sheet pan, cover with plastic that has one vent hole.

TO SERVE, cut with a cookie cutter or cocktail glass in the shape you like and pan sear on both sides until internal temperature reaches 140 degrees.

***Serves 6***

# Peach Soy Marinade

This is a wonderful, sweet, and full-flavored marinade that is especially delicious when used with chicken or pork. Do not marinate chicken or pork for more than 6 hours, as the soy and vinegar will toughen the meat.

## Ingredients

- *8 ounces peach nectar*
- *½ cup cider vinegar*
- *½ cup soy sauce*
- *½ cup ruby Port*
- *½ cup peach or apricot jam*
- *¼ cup Worcestershire sauce*
- *¼ cup fresh garlic, minced*
- *¼ cup hoisin sauce*
- *¼ teaspoon cayenne pepper*
- *¼ teaspoon black pepper*

## Preparation

COMBINE all ingredients, reserve until needed. Marinate the chicken or pork and grill.

***Yield: 4 cups***

*Wine suggestion: Terra Blanca 2001 Viogner*

# Stuffed Double Pork Chops

This recipe is perfect served with the Wild Mushroom Risotto, and lends itself well to either a spicy Zinfandel or a big Chardonnay.

## Ingredients

*4 cloves roasted garlic*
*6 ounces goat cheese*
*3 tablespoons fresh basil, chiffonade*
*2 tablespoons sun-dried tomatoes*
*6 12-ounce pork chops, thick cut, frenched*
*5 tablespoons of olive oil*
*salt and pepper to taste*
*wine or liquor (optional)*
*butter (optional)*

## Preparation

IN A small bowl, smash the garlic with a fork. Add the goat cheese, basil, sun-dried tomatoes, and mix well.

ON THE back of the chop, use a paring knife to cut a hole and slide the blade into the center of the chop. Keeping the butt of the knife stationary, so as not to widen the opening, rock the knife back and forth inside the chop, creating a pocket. After you have finished pocketing all of the chops, use your index finger and stuff a tablespoon of the stuffing into each of the chops.

HEAT the oven to 450 degrees. Heat a skillet with olive oil over medium high heat. Season the chops with salt and pepper and place them in the pan. Sear them on each side until browned and place in the oven for approximately 20 minutes, or until the internal temperature is 145 degrees. At this point you may remove the chops from the pan, pour off the oil, deglaze the pan with wine or liquor, and add some butter to make a sauce.

LET rest for 2-3 minutes and serve.

***Serves 6***

*Wine Suggestion: Rosenblum Cellars – Annette's Vineyard 1999, or Tandem Chardonaay – Ritchie Vineyard 2002*

# The Wine Spectator Award

Many of the restaurants included in this cookbook have been recognized by Wine Spectator, the world's most popular wine magazine. It reviews more than 10,000 wines each year and covers travel, fine dining and the lifestyle of wine for novices and connoisseurs alike. Through its Restaurant Awards program, the magazine recognizes restaurants around the world that offer distinguished wine lists.

Awards are given in three tiers. In 2003, more than 3,600 restaurants earned wine list awards. To qualify, wine lists must provide vintages and appellations for all selections. The overall presentation and appearance of the list are also important. Once past these initial requirements, lists are then judged for one of three awards: the Award of Excellence, the Best of Award of Excellence, and the Grand Award.

- Award of Excellence—The basic Award of Excellence recognizes restaurants with lists that offer a well-chosen selection of quality producers, along with a thematic match to the menu in both price and style.
- Best of Award of Excellence—The second-tier Best of Award of Excellence was created to give special recognition to those restaurants that exceed the requirements of the basic category. These lists must display vintage depth, including vertical offerings of several top wines, as well as excellent breadth from major wine growing regions.
- Grand Award—The highest award, the Grand Award, is given to those restaurants that show an uncompromising, passionate devotion to quality. These lists show serious depth of mature vintages, outstanding breadth in their vertical offerings, excellent harmony with the menu, and superior organization and presentation. In 2003, only 89 restaurants held Wine Spectator Grand Awards.

# *Bonsai Bistro*

101 E. Sherman Avenue
Coeur d'Alene, ID 83814
208-765-4321
www.cdaresort.com

Serving Daily
Winter months 11:00am to 10:00pm
Summer months 11:00am to 11:00pm

# Bonsai Bistro

***Troy Louis Chandler, Executive Chef/ General Manager***
***Steve Mitchell, Senior Sous Chef***
***Travis Whiteside, Sushi Chef***

The Coeur d'Alene area of Idaho is one of the most beautiful areas of the state, and a popular area for those who love water sports with the sparkling Lake Coeur d'Alene as a centerpiece. Situated on the north shore of the lake, overlooking Independence Point is the Bonsai Bistro, offering the finest in Pan-Asian Cuisine.

The building in which the restaurant is housed was originally built for a bank, but the architecture incorporated a Japanese style that makes it perfect for an Asian-influence restaurant. Done in classic Japanese décor, the serenity of Asian hospitality enfolds you. The upper dining room has a beautiful rock garden as its centerpiece. The tables are spaciously arranged, and the tables along the floor to ceiling windows offer nice views of Independence Point, the Coeur d'Alene Resort and the lake. The downstairs is unique in that it has slanted windows that open it to the natural light. It also features an outdoor patio set in a Japanese garden with a running river and a small waterfall and a Koi pond.

There is also a private dining room where you can enjoy a true culinary experience with a Chef's Table. Offered for parties of eight to fourteen, the chef will prepare a marvelous selection of Pan Asian cuisine. Bonsai Bistro describes its cuisine as fifty percent regional Chinese cuisine with a mix of Thai, Vietnamese, and Japanese sushi. The new Sushi Bar features fresh fish flown in daily, and all beef used in the restaurant is succulent Kobe beef. The full bar offers a fine selection found in most upscale restaurants, but supplements it with several types of Japanese sake as well as Japanese beer that complements the spicy nature of many of the dishes.

Executive Chef Troy Chandler describes Bonsai Bistro as a family-style restaurant with food that is meant to share. When you consider the extensive offerings on the menu, you will find this an appropriate concept since you will have a difficult time in choosing just one or two items. One other unique concept is the availability of take-out orders of anything on the menu. They deliver not only to your accommodations but also to dockside for those tied up at the marinas on the lake.

# Thai Hot and Sour Soup

As an option, you can finish this soup with a little peanut oil and Thai fish sauce for a unique, exotic flavor.

## Ingredients

- *peanut or vegetable oil*
- 1 *stalk lemon grass, halved & then cut in 1-inch pieces*
- 1 *tablespoon ginger, minced*
- 1 *cup crimini mushrooms, sliced*
- 3 *tablespoons Madras curry powder*
- 1 *cup green onions, white part only, ¼-inch dice*
- ½ *pound 26-30 tiger shrimp*
- 1 *quart chicken stock*
- 1 *cup water chestnuts, sliced*
- 1 *tablespoon Sriracha chili sauce*
- 1 *13.5 ounce can Chaokoh coconut milk*
- 3 *Roma tomatoes, large dice*
- *juice of 3 limes*
- ¼ *Thai basil leaves, torn*
- *salt and pepper to taste*
- *Thai fish sauce, optional for finish*
- *Peanut oil, optional for finish*

## Preparation

IN A large pot, heat enough peanut or vegetable oil and sauté lemon grass, ginger, mushrooms, curry powder, green onions, and shrimp, until shrimp are half cooked. Add chicken stock, water chestnuts, and chili sauce. Bring to a simmer and continue simmering for 10 minutes. Add coconut milk and simmer for 5 minutes. Add tomatoes, lime juice, and basil. Season to taste. Finish with a little peanut oil and Thais fish sauce, if desired.

***Serves 4 - 6***

# THAI CURRY PEANUT PRAWNS

The Thai Curry Peanut Sauce is best prepared at least 4 hours in advance, and chilled to thicken it. You can also substitute chicken for the prawns for a nice variation on this dish.

## Ingredients

*2 tablespoons vegetable oil*
*2 pounds tiger prawns*
*2 carrots, sliced thin*
*4 stalks bok choy, cut on bias*
*1 yellow onion, cut in 1-inch squares*
*1 teaspoon garlic, minced*
*Thai Curry Peanut Sauce (recipe follows)*
*cilantro sprigs, for garnish*
*1 lime, cut into 6 wedges, for garnish*
*red pepper, julienned, for garnish*
*roasted peanuts, for garnish*

## Preparation

IN A hot sauté pan or wok, add oil and stir-fry prawns, vegetables, and garlic until prawns are red. Add enough Thai Curry Peanut Sauce to generously coat all, and cook on medium for 1 minute.

TO SERVE, garnish each plate with cilantro, red pepper, peanuts, and a wedge of fresh lime.

***Serves 6 – 8***

## For the Thai Curry Peanut Sauce

*¼ cup black tea leaves*
*1½ cups chicken stock, scalding hot*
*cooking oil*
*4 green onions, cut on bias*
*1 tablespoon garlic, minced*
*1 tablespoon ginger minced*
*3 tablespoons Madras curry powder*
*chicken stock, to make paste*
*2 cups coconut milk*
*½ cup lime juice*
*¼ cup honey*
*¼ cup Thai fish sauce*
*1 cup chunky peanut butter*

ADD tea leaves to scalding hot chicken stock and let steep. In a hot wok or sauté pan, sauté green onions, garlic, and ginger in a small amount of cooking oil. Over medium heat, add curry powder and just enough chicken stock to make a paste. Cook this for 1 minute. Add the rest of the ingredients and cook over low heat for 5 minutes, stirring constantly. Strain the tea-infused chicken stock, discarding the tea leaves, and add the stock to the sauce. Set aside, and chill to thicken sauce. This should be done at least 4 hours before using in the recipe.

# Crispy Salmon with Black Bean Sauce

## Ingredients

- 2 *pounds fresh wild salmon*
- 1 *cup potato or corn starch, seasoned with sea salt & white pepper*
- 4 *cups soybean or canola oil*
- *Black Bean Sauce (recipe follows)*
- 3 *cups cooked jasmine rice*
- ¼ *cup green onion, chopped*
- ¼ *cup red pepper, fine dice*
- *cilantro sprigs, for garnish*

## Preparation

CUT salmon into 1-inch by 4-inch pieces. Lightly dust pieces with seasoned starch. Heat oil in a wok to 425 degrees. Carefully drop salmon into heated oil, one piece at a time. With a metal spatula, gently stir salmon away from you to separate. Cook for 1 minute.

Turn off heat and remove salmon, placing on paper towels to drain. Put in warm oven to keep hot. Pour oil into holding container and let cool. Do not rinse wok, as it will be used to make Black Bean Sauce.

TO SERVE, mix cooked rice, green onions, and red pepper. Ladle enough Black Bean Sauce onto plates to cover the entire plate. Place a scoop of the rice mix onto the center of each plate. Place salmon around rice mound and top with cilantro garnish.

***Serves 4***

## For the Black Bean Sauce

- ¼ *cup Chinese preserved black beans*
- 1 *tablespoon garlic, minced*
- 1 *tablespoon ginger, minced*
- 3 *cups soy sauce*
- 1 *cup Mi Chiu rice wine*
- ⅓ *cup oyster sauce*
- 1 *cup sugar*
- ½ *cup mushroom soy sauce*
- 2½ *cups chicken stock*
- 1 *cup slurry (equal parts cornstarch & cold water)*

OVER medium heat, add black beans, garlic, and ginger to the un-rinsed wok (see above). Stir fry, smashing the black beans to release their power. Add all sauce ingredients except the slurry. Bring to a simmer, and add slurry 1 tablespoon at a time until sauce thickens to a bubbling state.

# Spicy Thai Mint Chicken

## Ingredients

- 1 *rhizome of ginger, smashed*
- 1 *gallon water*
- 3 *pounds chicken breast, sliced*
- 3 *tablespoons vegetable oil*
- 3 *tablespoons peanut oil*
- 36 *dried red chili pods*
- 1 *pound white mushrooms, quartered*
- 1 *small yellow onion, cut to 1-inch dice*
- 1 *bunch green onions, cut on bias to 1-inch pieces*
- 1 *tablespoon garlic, minced*
- 1 *tablespoon ginger, minced*
- ¼ *cup chili paste (Sambal Olek or Sriracha)*
- 4 *Roma tomatoes, cot to 1-inch dice*
- *Oyster-Mushroom Sauce (recipe follows)*
- 1 *cup slurry (equal parts cornstarch and cold water)*
- 1 *cup mint, chopped*

## Preparation

PLACE smashed ginger in the water and bring to a simmer. Poach chicken slices in the simmering ginger broth until fully cooked. Strain chicken and discard broth.

IN A hot wok, add vegetable oil and peanut oil along with chili pods. Stir-fry chili pods until they have a roasted mahogany color. Add mushrooms, onions, and chicken. Stir-fry until the yellow onions are translucent. Add minced garlic, ginger, and chili paste, stir-frying briefly. Add tomatoes and enough Oyster-Mushroom Sauce to coat. Add more sauce based on individual preference. Simmer for 30 seconds. Add 1 tablespoon of slurry at a time until sauce is desired consistency. Stir in most of the mint, leaving enough to garnish each plate.

***Serves 4 – 6***

## For the Oyster-Mushroom Sauce

- 1½ *cups soy sauce*
- ½ *cup Mi Chiu Rice Wine*
- ¼ *cup oyster sauce*
- ½ *cup sugar*
- ¼ *cup mushroom soy sauce*
- 1¼ *cups chicken stock*

COMBINE ingredients and set aside.

# *Brix*

317 Sherman Avenue
Coeur d'Alene, ID 83814
208-665-7407
www.brixrestaurant.com

Lunch daily 11:00am to 2:00pm
Dinner Sunday – Thursday
5:00pm to 9:00pm
Friday – Saturday 5:00pm to
10:00pm

# *Brix*

***Jerry Goggin, Owner***
***Paul D'Orazi, Manager***
***Adam Hegsted, Executive Chef***
***Erik Johnson, Sous Chef***

Located in a landmark downtown building, Brix is an event all its own. The three-story brick building was built in 1905 and was the former home of J.C. Penney's. The original brick walls, classic tin ceiling, and rustic hardwood floors have been incorporated into the design of the restaurant, along with hand-blown glass lighting and dark wood furniture. The elegant centerpiece of the non-smoking dining room is a spectacular silk chandelier. The restaurant also features intimate dining on the mezzanine for parties up to 35, and can also accommodate private parties up to 100 in the downstairs banquet facility. Along with the upscale dining scene, Brix also features a lounge on the first floor that is a favorite of locals.

Executive Chef Adam Hegsted has a passion: It's food. It's what he loves to do. At Brix, he has created an eclectic menu using the freshest seasonal ingredients. He uses simple big flavors and puts them together in an interesting way. On every plate, Chef Hegsted balances all elements of taste, smell, texture, and visual appeal. The menu changes seasonally to reflect what is available locally and in the Northwest, from the wild morels and huckleberries of the Idaho forests to the Washington farmed asparagus and Alaskan salmon. A daily menu is produced showcasing the fresh seafood that is available, with the preparations changing day by day. You will also find an extensive selection of regional and imported wines to complement your culinary choices.

Chef Hegsted developed his food passion when he started as a dishwasher to earn some side cash. He attended Inland Northwest Culinary Academy in Spokane to develop his basic culinary knowledge and then went to the Art Institute of Seattle. Before coming to Brix, he cooked for the potential members of the exclusive Black Rock Country Club as well as for the owner. While filling the position of Executive Chef at Cedars Restaurant in Coeur d'Alene, he also apprenticed at the California Club in Los Angeles under Chef Jean Marc Weber. At Brix, Chef Hegsted has developed his own culinary philosophy: one of preparing simple food, using classic techniques in new and innovative ways.

# Rock Crab Cake

*with Citrus Aioli and Shaved Fennel-Orange Salad*

## Ingredients

- *5 pounds rock crab*
- *½ red bell pepper, chopped fine*
- *½ red onion, chopped fine*
- *½ cup celery, chopped*
- *½ tablespoon garlic, chopped*
- *½ cup parsley, chopped*
- *¼ cup Dijon mustard*
- *1 cup mayonnaise*
- *2 eggs*
- *4 cups Panko*
- *½ cup cream*
- *4 tablespoons seafood seasoning*
- *2 tablespoon salt*
- *2 tablespoons pepper*
- *1 tablespoon dry mustard*
- *standard breading ingredients: flour, egg wash, Panko*
- *oil for deep frying*
- *Citrus Aioli (recipe follows)*
- *Shaved Fennel-Orange Salad (recipe follows)*

## Preparation

FOLD all of the ingredients together, except the breading ingredients and the oil. Taking about 2 ounces of the mixture, shape it into a crab cake. Repeat with the rest.

HEAT oil to 350 degrees in a large, deep pot and deep-fry the crab cakes in batches until golden. Remove crab cakes and keep warm in oven.

TO SERVE, place Shaved Fennel-Orange Salad in center of a large serving platter. Place crab cakes around the salad, and drizzle Citrus Aioli over the cakes.

## For the Citrus Aioli

- *4 egg yolks*
- *1 teaspoon Dijon mustard*
- *1 teaspoon paprika*
- *3 cloves garlic, minced*
- *½ teaspoon salt*
- *½ teaspoon pepper*
- *¼ cup lemon juice*
- *1 lime, squeezed*
- *1 orange, squeezed*
- *2 cups olive oil*

COMBINE all ingredients except the oil. Slowly drizzle in oil until emulsified.

## For the Shaved Fennel-Orange Salad

- *1 fennel bulb, shaved*
- *2 oranges, peeled, sliced, & seeded*
- *1 bunch watercress, rough chopped*
- *3 tablespoons sugar*
- *1 tablespoon canola oil*
- *3 tablespoons lemon juice*
- *1 teaspoon salt*
- *1 teaspoon pepper*

FOLD all ingredients together and let marinate 1 hour before serving.

***Yield: 40 2-ounce cakes***

*Wine suggestion: Rombauer Chardonnay-Carneros*

# Baby Spinach Salad

*with Warm Bacon Vinaigrette, Potato Frites, and Dried Cherries and Poached Fried Egg*

This is our version of the Classic Spinach Salad. The dressing is sort of sweet and sour, and brings all the elements of this salad together very well.

## Ingredients

- *2 pounds baby spinach*
- *1 cup applewood smoked bacon, rendered and diced (bacon fat reserved)*
- *1 cup dried tart cherries*
- *1 cup Maytag blue cheese, crumbled*
- *1 cup Potato Frites (recipe follows)*
- *Bacon Vinaigrette (recipe follows)*
- *Poached Fried Egg (recipe follows)*

## Preparation

SAVE reserved bacon fat for vinaigrette. Gently toss the rest of the ingredients together and dress with Bacon Vinaigrette. To serve, place on salad plates and sprinkle a few Potato Frites over top. Gently place fried egg on top.

***Serves 10***

*Wine suggestion: 2004 Chenin Blanc, L'Ecole, Walla Walla, Washington*

## For the Potato Frites

- *Red potatoes, julienned*
- *Oil for deep-frying*

HEAT oil to 300 degrees; add julienned potatoes and fry until crisp. Remove from oil, and drain.

## For the Bacon Vinaigrette

- *1 tablespoon Dijon mustard*
- *¼ cup honey*
- *¼ cup maple syrup*
- *¼ tablespoon salt*
- *¼ tablespoon pepper*
- *1 clove garlic, minced*
- *1 shallot, minced*
- *¼ cup rendered bacon, diced*
- *½ cup balsamic vinegar*
- *1½ tablespoons Worcestershire*
- *¾ cup apple cider vinegar*
- *1½ cups warm bacon fat*
- *1 cup olive oil*

SET aside the bacon fat and olive oil. Combine all the other ingredients in blender. Slowly drizzle in the bacon fat and olive oil while blending. Serve immediately, or keep warm.

## For the Poached Fried Eggs

- 10 *eggs*
- *white vinegar for poaching*
- 4 *cups flour*
- 2 *tablespoons pepper*
- 2 *tablespoons salt*
- 1 *teaspoon paprika*
- *oil for frying*

HEAT fryer to 350 degrees. Mix flour, pepper, salt, and paprika together. Get an ice water bath ready for eggs. Put 2 inches of water into a pot and bring to a low simmer. Add a little salt and white vinegar to the water. Crack eggs into a shallow cup. Slowly lower into simmering water and poach 2-3 minutes, until you can pick them up with a kitchen spoon. When cooked, place gently into ice bath and cool for ten minutes. Remove eggs and dry as much as possible. Add one egg at a time and gently dredge in flour mixture. Shake off excess. Fry for one-two minutes until slightly crisp. Set aside to cool slightly.

*Couer d'Alene ca. 1893*

# Honey-Cider Brined Pork Chop

*with Braised Cabbage, Blue Cheese Macaroni, and Port Reduction*

These are some of the best pork chops I've tasted. The brine makes these chops very moist and tender. The macaroni and cabbage also complement this dish very well.

## Ingredients

*8 double cut pork chops, frenched*
*8 ounces salt*
*8 ounces sugar*
*8 ounces honey*
*5 bay leaves*
*8 cloves*
*½ tablespoon mustard seed*
*¼ stick cinnamon*
*2 bunches thyme*
*10 peppercorns*
*2 cups cider*
*4 cups hot water*
*¼ cup melted butter (reserve for glazing)*
*Braised Cabbage (recipe follows)*
*Port Reduction (recipe follows)*
*Blue Cheese Macaroni (recipe follows)*
*Spice Roasted Apple (recipe follows)*

## Preparation

MIX the brine ingredients together (salt through hot water), and add the pork chops. Brine the chops for 4 to 12 hours.

HEAT grill to medium-low heat. Remove chops from brine and pat dry. Grill each pork chop at low heat until cooked to 145 degrees, about 35 minutes. When finished, glaze with melted butter, and let rest for 10 minutes.

TO SERVE, place a pork chop in the center of each individual plate. On one side of the chop, place a portion of Braised Cabbage, and on the other side place the Blue Cheese Macaroni. Drizzle the Port Reduction over the pork chop. Place Spice Roasted Apple on top of cabbage.

## For the Spice Roasted Apple

*2 Braeburn apples*
*1 teaspoon nutmeg*
*1 teaspoon pepper*
*1 teaspoon sugar*
*pinch salt*
*1 teaspoon canola oil*

HEAT oven to 400 degrees. Mix spices with oil. Peel and core apples. Cut into quarters and toss into spices. Place on a pan and roast for 10 minutes, until light golden.

## For the Braised Cabbage

*1 head purple cabbage, sliced thin*
*½ cup canola oil*
*1 cup apple cider vinegar*
*1 cup red wine*
*1 cup sugar*
*½ cup chicken stock*
*1 clove garlic, crushed*
*salt & pepper to taste*

SAUTÉ the cabbage in the oil until wilted. Add rest of the ingredients and cook down until almost dry. Keep warm.

## For the Port Reduction

*1 bottle port*
*2 cups chicken stock*
*1 pig trotter (pig's foot, if not available any pork bone will work)*
*1 cup sugar*
*1 tablespoon pepper*
*1 tablespoon salt*
*1 stick cinnamon*

SIMMER all ingredients until the mixture is reduced to a light syrup. Remove and discard the pig trotter. Keep warm.

## For the Blue Cheese Macaroni

*4 cups blue cheese, divided*
*2 cups breadcrumbs*
*½ cup Parmesan cheese*
*2 cups melted butter*
*½ cup clarified butter*
*1 cup flour*
*½ sweet onion, diced*
*2 quarts heavy cream, warmed*
*1 teaspoon nutmeg*
*1 teaspoon garlic, crushed*
*1 teaspoon chili flakes*
*1 tablespoon ground black pepper*
*3½ tablespoons salt*
*½ pound mozzarella*
*½ pound butter*
*1 gallon cooked and chilled macaroni*

HEAT oven to 400 degrees. Make the topping by combining 2 cups of the blue cheese with the breadcrumbs, Parmesan cheese, and melted butter. Set aside. Cook clarified butter and flour for 2 minutes. Add onion and sweat. Add warmed cream to the flour mix while stirring. Add all spices and simmer for 10 minutes. Turn off the heat and add butter, mozzarella, and remaining 2 cups of blue cheese. Pour mixture over macaroni and put into individual serving dishes. Top with a little of the breadcrumb mixture and bake until golden, about 5-8 minutes.

***Yield: 8 4.5-ounce servings***

*Wine suggestion: 2004 Zinfandel, M. Consentino, "Cigarzin", Lodi California*

# Long Bone Short Ribs

*with Gremolata and Horseradish Mashed Potatoes*

This is an unusual cut of beef, but is fairly inexpensive. Ask for the first three ribs of the chuck, cut two inches thick, and seven to nine inches long. It is a fairly simple dish with rich and layered flavors.

## Ingredients

- *8 pounds long bone short ribs*
- *salt*
- *¼ cup olive oil*
- *2 stalks celery, chopped*
- *½ sweet onion, chopped*
- *2 garlic cloves, smashed*
- *2 tablespoons flour*
- *1 bottle cabernet sauvignon*
- *3 cups veal stock*
- *¼ cup sugar*
- *Horseradish Mashed Potatoes (recipe follows)*
- *Gremolata (recipe follows)*
- *Horseradish Aioli (recipe follows)*

## Preparation

SALT short ribs and let rest for at least 4 hours.

HEAT oven to 350 degrees. In a large, ovenproof braising pan, sear the short ribs in the olive oil until golden. Remove from pan and set aside. Add celery and onions, and brown. Add garlic and flour and sweat, stirring to combine. Return ribs to pan and add wine and stock. Bring to a simmer, cover, and place in 350-degree oven for 3 to 4 hours, until fork tender.

TO SERVE, place Horseradish Mashed Potatoes on individual plates along with a serving of short ribs. Spoon short rib sauce over ribs, and top with the Gremolata. Drizzle Horseradish Aioli on plates.

***Serves 5 – 8***

*Wine suggestion: 2002 Stella Maris Red Wine, Columbia Valley, Washington*

## For the Horseradish Mashed Potatoes

- *4 pounds russet potatoes, peeled*
- *1 tablespoon roasted garlic*
- *½ cup horseradish purée*
- *1 cup hot cream*
- *½ pound butter, melted*
- *1 teaspoon lemon juice*
- *salt and pepper to taste*

BOIL potatoes in salted water until done. Drain, and let dry in warm oven. Put dried potatoes through ricer and whip. Add garlic, horseradish, hot cream, and butter, mixing until combined. Add lemon juice and season with salt and pepper. Keep warm until ready to serve.

## For the Gremolata

- ¼ cup lemon zest, shredded on micro plane
- ¼ cup fresh horseradish, shredded
- 1 tablespoon garlic, minced
- ¼ cup Italian parsley, julienne
- ½ teaspoon sugar
- pinch salt

MIX together and hold for service.

## For the Horseradish Aioli

- 4 egg yolks
- 1 teaspoon Dijon mustard
- 1 teaspoon paprika
- 3 clove garlic
- ½ tablespoon salt
- ½ tablespoon pepper
- ½ cup lemon juice
- ½ cup horseradish
- 3 cup olive oil

IN A blender, mix everything but the olive oil. Blend for 30 seconds. While blender is on, slowly drizzle in oil. If it gets too thick, add water to thin. Reserve for service.

*Couer d'Alene Boat Club Regatta ca. 1910*

# *The Wine Cellar*

313 Sherman Avenue
Coeur d'Alene, ID 83854
208-664-WINE (664-9463)
www.coeurdalenewinecellar.com

Dinner Monday – Thursday 4:30pm to 10:00pm
Friday – Saturday 4:30pm to 12:00am
Music Tuesday – Thursday 7:00pm to 10:00pm
Friday – Saturday 8:00pm to 12:00am

# The Wine Cellar

***Jim Duncan, Owner***
***Cheryl Callins, Chef de Cuisine***

After a day on the beach in the bright Idaho sun, tripping down the steps to the Wine Cellar's subterranean location and spending the evening in the softly illuminated restaurant is a treat for the eyes as well as the palate. The old stone foundation walls are exposed to give the room a unique feel and it is divided by a set of Mediterranean style arches, making the space more intimate. Along with a great meal, guests can enjoy a constantly rotating group of bands that feature jazz and blues. Both meals and music can be enjoyed as late as midnight on both Fridays and Saturdays.

The restaurant has been a mainstay of the Coeur d'Alene scene for many years, and owner Jim Duncan makes sure that the quality of the food and wine continues to stay high. While steaks and wild salmon with a Pacific Rim influence are delicious choices on the menu, the restaurant features the Mediterranean influence of France and Italy in most of its dishes. A traditional bouillabaisse from Marseilles is a signature dish, and the menu offers platters for two or more diners including a house specialty, Basque-style paella. A unique treat is the value-priced three-course meals that are offered featuring the restaurant's Mediterranean dishes. You can start with a choice of housemade potato gnocchi or linguini served with two types of sauces. This is followed by an entrée, such as lamb shank with portobello polenta or chicken breast stuffed with chèvre, artichoke hearts, and sun-dried tomatoes and topped off with a sun-dried tomato cream sauce. Finish your meal with a choice of a salad, assorted cheeses with apple slices, or a luscious house-made dessert.

Jim chose the name of his restaurant with care. As an avid enophile, Jim immersed himself in the wines of the world. His wine list features over 250 selections from California and the Northwest, to Australia, France, Spain, New Zealand, South Africa, and Italy. His frequent trips to France, Spain, Portugal, and Italy have increased his knowledge of wines. The restaurant has won Wine Spectator magazine's Award of Excellence along with their Distinguished Dining Award. It has also been named as Idaho's Outstanding Wine List twice by Northwest Wine Press magazine.

# Bouillabaisse Marseilles

This can be made with just about any kind of seafood that you choose, including mussels, clams, and calamari. Make the base first, and then add your choice of fish at the end, cooking just until mussels and clams open and seafood is cooked through.

## Ingredients

- 12 *pounds fish and/or seafood, your choice*
- 10 *cups potatoes, ½-inch dice*
- 2 *cups yellow onion, julienne*
- 2 *cups green peppers, medium dice*
- ½ *cup olive oil*
- 4 *quarts clam stock*
- ½ *cup garlic, minced*
- 1 *rounded tablespoon dried basil*
- 1 *teaspoon saffron threads*
- ½ *cup sugar*
- 1 *#10 can diced tomatoes in juice*
- 3 *cups red wine*
- 1 *rounded tablespoon red pepper flakes*
- *Rouille (recipe follows*
- *toasted croutons for garnish*

## Preparation

STEAM the diced potatoes until they are al dente. Set aside to cool.

IN A large stockpot, sauté the onions and green peppers in the olive oil until onion is translucent. Cut the diced tomatoes into smaller chunks and add them to the mixture, along with all other ingredients except the potatoes. Bring mixture to a simmer and cook at a slow simmer for 30 minutes. Add your choice of seafood and cook just until done. If any clams or mussels do not open up, discard them. Add potatoes at the end, so that they do not get too mushy.

TO SERVE, ladle into soup bowls and top with a few croutons. Serve the Rouille on the side.

***Serves 24***

*Wine suggestions: an Oregon Pinto Gris or an Italian Pinot Grigio*

## For the Rouille

- ½ *cup fresh garlic cloves*
- 4 *cups mayonnaise*
- 1 *tablespoon salt*
- 2 *teaspoons cayenne pepper*
- 1 *tablespoon paprika*
- ½ *cup lemon juice*
- 2 *cups roasted red bell peppers*

IN A food processor, blend all ingredients until completely incorporated into a thick sauce.

# Roasted Tomato Boursin Tart with Salsa Garni

## Ingredients

*4 tablespoons butter*
*1 tablespoon shortening*
*1 cup flour*
*cold water*
*2 tablespoons toasted pine nuts, coarse chopped*
*4 large tomatoes, sliced ½-inch thick*
*4 large garlic cloves, minced*
*salt and pepper to taste*
*¼ cup olive oil*
*1 cup ricotta*
*1 5.2-ounce package Boursin cheese*
*1 egg, separated*
*2 tablespoons fresh basil, minced*
*Salsa Garni (recipe follows)*

## Preparation

IN A bowl, cut together the butter, shortening, and flour. Add a tablespoon at a time of cold water until dough forms right consistency. Wrap in plastic and chill in refrigerator for 1 hour.

HEAT oven to 350 degrees. Put tomato slices on sheet pan. Sprinkle with salt and pepper and garlic. Drizzle with olive oil and roast in oven until tomatoes have lost most of their water content, about 20 minutes. Remove from oven.

RAISE oven temperature to 425 degrees. Roll out dough to form a crust for a 10-inch tart pan. Brush with egg wash, using the separated egg yolk, and pre-bake crust in the 425-degree oven for 15 minutes. Lower oven temperature to 350 degrees.

IN A bowl, combine the ricotta and Boursin with the egg white. Layer roasted tomatoes in the pre-baked crust. Top with cheese mix and bake in 350-degree oven for 35 minutes.

TO SERVE, cut tart into individual portions and top with Salsa Garni.

***Serves 12 as a appetizer***

*Wine suggestion: an apéritif wine such as a sauterne or muscato*

## For the Salsa Garni

*2 Roma tomatoes, coarse chop*
*2 tablespoons fresh basil, chopped*
*1 pinch of salt*
*1 tablespoon olive oil*

COMBINE tomato, basil, and salt in a bowl. Drizzle with olive oil, tossing to coat.

# Lamb Shank Osso Bucco

*with Portobello Polenta*

## Ingredients

- 16 *lamb shanks*
- *flour*
- *salt and pepper*
- 2 *large yellow onions, sliced thin*
- 2 *cups carrots, sliced thin*
- 2 *cups celery, sliced thin*
- 2 *tablespoons garlic, minced*
- ½ *pound margarine*
- 1 *#10 can diced tomatoes*
- 3 *cups white wine*
- 3 *bay leaves*
- 1 *tablespoon basil*
- 1 *tablespoon thyme*
- ¼ *cup beef base*
- *Portobello Polenta (recipe follows)*

## Preparation

HEAT oven to 325 degrees. Flour, salt, and pepper the shanks and roast in a hotel pan in the oven for 1 hour. Remove from oven and raise temperature to 350 degrees.

WHILE shanks are roasting, sauté the onions, carrots, celery, and garlic in the margarine until the onions are translucent. In a large pot, place the tomatoes, wine, bay leaves, basil, thyme, and beef base and bring to a boil.

POUR onion mixture over roasted shanks, and then pour tomato mixture over all, stirring to combine and to make sure the shanks are coated with the vegetables. Cover and bake in 350-degree oven for about 45 minutes, or until meat is ready to fall off the bone.

SERVE with Portobello Polenta.

***Serves 16***

*Wine suggestion: a big Italian red, such as Amarone or Brunello*

## For the Portobello Polenta

- 3 *large portobello mushrooms, ⅜-inch dice*
- *olive oil*
- 1 *quart mushroom stock*
- 1 *quart vegetable or chicken stock*
- 1 *quart milk*
- 6 *cups cornmeal*
- 6 *cups water*

HEAT oven to 350 degrees. Place the mushroom dice in a roasting pan and drizzle with a little olive oil, tossing to coat. Roast mushrooms in oven for about 10 – 12 minutes. In a heavy stockpot, heat mushroom and chicken stock. When hot, add milk and bring back to heated temperature. Meanwhile, mix the cornmeal and water together. When milk and stock mixture is hot, whisk in the cornmeal mix and stir constantly, until it pulls away from the sides of the pot. Pour into a 4-inch full hotel pan and stir in the roasted mushrooms. Keep warm for service.

*Couer d'Alene Bicycle Club ca. 1895*

# Red Door

215 S. Main Street
Moscow, ID 83843
208-882-7830
www.red-door-restaurant.com

Dinner
Tuesday – Saturday
5:30pm to 9:30pm

# Red Door

### *Jeanne Clothiaux and Tracy Wright, Owners*
### *Hal Jardine, Chef/Owner*
### *Ian Dickinson, Sous Chef*

Moscow, Idaho is located in the north central portion of the state in what is known as the Palouse, named after the indigenous tribe of Indians. The undulating hills of the Palouse serve as a beautiful agricultural part of the state where an abundance of wheat, dry peas, and lentils are harvested. The first settlers arrived in 1871, and the first store was opened on what is now Main Street in 1875, and the town was chosen as the site for what would become the University of Idaho shortly thereafter. Washington State University is situated just eight miles away, in Pullman, Washington. The vibrancy of the communities shows in the music and art that abounds, along with the great outdoor opportunities available. Such an atmosphere attracted Jeanne Clothiaux and her business partner, Tracy Wright, to the area where they established a restaurant in 1998 that is well loved by the locals and also attracts the many visitors to the area. The bright red door on tree-lined Main Street is easily spotted and, in the evenings, you can see happy diners enjoying their meals by candlelight.

Jeanne Clothiaux grew up in the South, with her father's side of the family coming from southern Louisiana. She was introduced to the spicy style of Cajun food at a young age and remembers the wonderful times when the family gathered in the kitchen to talk and cook. Those culinary roots taught her the value of using fresh, local ingredients and taking time to prepare dishes correctly. Both she and Chef Jardine are subscribers to the slow food movement, and believe in using fresh vegetables, cut by hand, and sauces made from homemade stocks. These labor-intensive methods show in the wonderful sauces and preserves you will find on the menu.

If slow food is your thing, you will love the Seven Hour Leg of Lamb. This requires an advance notice of 48 hours and serves four people. Local produce and meats are used whenever possible, getting their lamb from nearby Rosebrush Farm and their elk sausage from Lone Hawk Farms. The Moscow Food Co-op bakes their breads, and the restaurant's wine list features many wines from the Northwest as well as Merlot from nearby Camas Prairie Winery.

# Beef Tenderloin Filet

*with Morel Cream Sauce and Asparagus*

Morels are gathered in late spring in the Moscow area. This dish can be made with fresh or dried morels.

## Ingredients

- *4 8-ounce beef tenderloin filets*
- *salt and freshly ground pepper to taste*
- *3 tablespoons unsalted butter, divided*
- *1 tablespoon vegetable oil*
- *20 pencil-sized asparagus, trimmed*
- *Morel Cream Sauce (recipe follows)*
- *¼ teaspoon Hungarian paprika*

## Preparation

HEAT oven to 350 degrees. Season steaks with salt and pepper. Heat 1 tablespoon of the butter along with the vegetable oil in a large sauté pan over medium-high heat. Sear steaks 2-3 minutes on each side to brown. Remove from pan and place on baking sheet in 350-degree oven to finish cooking, about 6 minutes for rare and 10 minutes for medium-rare. Drain and reserve searing pan for finishing sauce.

BLANCH asparagus, drain, and cut into 2-inch lengths. Heat 2 tablespoons butter in a sauté pan over medium-high heat. Add asparagus and sauté until just tender. Season with salt and keep warm for service.

TO SERVE, place each steak in the center of a large plate and nap with Morel Cream Sauce. Arrange asparagus around steaks and dust with paprika.

## For the Morel Cream Sauce

- *½ cup dried morels*
- *1½ cups chicken stock*
- *1 tablespoon unsalted butter*
- *1 leek, white part only, finely chopped*
- *¼ cup shallots, finely chopped*
- *1 teaspoon garlic, minced*
- *¼ cup dry white wine*
- *1 teaspoon fresh thyme leaves*
- *1½ cups cream*
- *1 tablespoon stone-ground mustard*
- *2 teaspoons fresh sage leaves, chopped*

REHYDRATE dried morels in chicken stock. Drain and set morels aside, reserving the liquid. Melt butter in a saucepan over medium-low heat. Add leeks, shallots, and garlic. Cover and sweat for 3 minutes. Add drained morels, white wine, and thyme. Increase heat and cook uncovered until most of the wine has evaporated. Add the reserved liquid and cream. Reduce by half and purée. Warm mixture gently in steak-searing pan and whisk in the mustard and sage just before serving. Adjust seasoning with salt and pepper.

***Serves 4***

*Wine suggestion: Clos du Val Cabernet Sauvignon 2002*

# Wild Alaskan Salmon

*with Mascarpone Cream Sauce, Lentils du Pays, and Sautéed Spinach*

Northwesterners love wild salmon. The rolling hills of the Palouse, where Moscow is cradled, produce a large percentage of the world's lentils. This recipe incorporates salmon and lentils into a hearty dish that's great for fall dinner parties.

## Ingredients

- *4 6-ounce wild salmon filets*
- *1 tablespoon vegetable oil*
- *sea salt and freshly ground black pepper to taste*
- *Lentils du Pays (recipe follows)*
- *Sautéed Spinach (recipe follows)*
- *Mascarpone Cream Sauce (recipe follows)*
- *½ cup basil, chiffonade*
- *4 lemon slices*

## Preparation

HEAT oven to 350 degrees. Season filets with salt and pepper. Heat oil over high heat and sear filets on each side to brown, about 2 minutes per side. Remove to baking sheet and place in hot oven to finish cooking, about 5 minutes. Salmon should be served medium-rare to medium.

TO SERVE, divide Lentils du Pays and its stock among 4 large pasta bowls. Divide Sautéed Spinach among the bowls, placing it in the center of each lentil mound. Place one salmon filet on each portion of spinach and nap with Mascarpone Cream Sauce. Garnish with lemon slices and basil.

***Serves 4***

*Wine suggestion: 2D Pinot Noir 2004*

## For the Lentils du Pays

- *4 cups chicken stock, divided*
- *¾ cup dry lentils*
- *½ teaspoon fresh thyme leaves*
- *1 bay leaf*
- *1 teaspoon garlic, minced*
- *1 tablespoon unsalted butter*
- *2 tablespoons carrot, fine dice*
- *2 tablespoons shallot, fine dice*
- *2 tablespoons celery, fine dice*
- *salt and white pepper to taste*

BRING 2 cups of the chicken stock and the lentils to a boil. Reduce heat and add thyme, bay leaf, and garlic. Cover and allow to simmer until tender, about 30 minutes. In a sauté pan, melt butter over medium low heat. Add carrots, shallots, and celery. Cover and sweat for about 3 minutes, to soften. Add to lentils. Warm remaining stock and add to lentils. Season with salt and pepper.

## For the Sautéed Spinach

- *2 tablespoons unsalted butter*
- *2 teaspoons garlic, minced*
- *1 pound fresh spinach leaves, washed*
- *½ teaspoon sea salt*

MELT butter over medium-high heat. Add garlic and immediately add spinach and salt. Cover. Turn off heat and allow to steam for 3 minutes.

## For the Mascarpone Cream Sauce

- *1 tablespoon unsalted butter*
- *¼ cup yellow onion, fine dice*
- *2 tablespoons carrot, fine dice*
- *1 teaspoon garlic, minced*
- *2 tablespoons fresh basil, finely chopped*
- *1 teaspoon lemon juice*
- *¼ cup chicken stock*
- *¼ cup mascarpone*
- *2 tablespoons Pecorino-Romano cheese, grated*
- *1 cup cream*

MELT butter over medium-low heat. Add onion, carrot, and garlic and sweat 3 minutes. Add basil, lemon juice, and chicken stock. Increase heat and reduce by half. Purée with mascarpone and Pecorino-Romano. Combine mixture with cream in a saucepan and simmer, whisking, until slightly thickened.

# Elk Loin

*with Brandied Raspberry Sauce and Spinach Quenelles*

We purchase farm-raised elk from Lonehawk Farm here in Moscow. The meat is lean and deep red.

## Ingredients

- *4 8-ounce Lonehawk Farm boneless elk loin chops*
- *salt and freshly ground black pepper*
- *2 tablespoons clarified butter*
- *2 tablespoons vegetable oil*
- *Brandied Raspberry Sauce (recipe follows)*
- *Spinach Quenelles (recipe follows)*

## Preparation

HEAT oven to 450 degrees. Season chops with salt and pepper. Heat butter and oil over medium-high heat in a large sauté pan. Add elk and sear each side for 3 minutes. Elk should be rare. If more cooking is desired, transfer to 450-degree oven.

TO SERVE, slice each steak into thin strips. Divide half of the Brandied Raspberry Sauce between 4 plates. Fan the elk slices over the sauce and nap with the remaining sauce. Place 2 quenelles on each plate alongside the sliced elk.

## For the Brandied Raspberry Sauce

- *1 Granny Smith apple, cored, and diced into ⅓-inch pieces*
- *½ cup brandy*
- *2 tablespoons sugar*
- *2 cups raspberries*
- *1 teaspoon fresh mint, chopped*
- *sea salt and white pepper to taste*
- *2 tablespoons cold butter, cut into small chunks*

COOK apples, brandy, and sugar to form a thick compote. Add raspberries and remove from heat. Add mint, season, and finish with butter, whisking in chunks piece by piece.

## For the Spinach Quenelles

- *1 pound fresh spinach leaves, washed*
- *½ cup packed parsley, trimmed of large stems*
- *¾ cup cream*
- *½ teaspoon sea salt*
- *2 teaspoons clarified butter, divided*

BLANCH spinach and parsley. Squeeze out all water by twisting in a cloth napkin. Purée with cream in a food processor to form a smooth paste. Season with salt. Heat ½ teaspoon of the butter in a sauté pan over medium-high heat. Add 3 tablespoons of spinach purée and sauté, tossing to heat through and form a football-shaped quenelle. Repeat with remainder of butter and spinach purée.

***Serves 4***

*Wine suggestion: Elderton Shiraz 2003*

# Epicurean
## At Hotel McCall

1101 N 3rd Street
McCall, ID 83638
208-634-8188


Dinner
Wednesday - Sunday
5:00pm to 9:00pm

# Epicurean

## *David Sefick and Sean Thueson, Owners and Chefs*

The charming little town of McCall, Idaho is a great place to visit both summer and winter. Situated on the shores of scenic Payette Lake sits the historic Hotel McCall that has been in operation since 1904. Inside the Hotel McCall you will find a delightful restaurant that has been owned by two chefs since December 2001. The food at the Epicurean is original, bright, and flavorful, with a variety of seafood, meat, and vegetarian dishes that show the influence of both chefs.

Chef Dave Sefick grew up in Salinas, California, famous for its lettuce, avocados, artichokes, vine ripened tomatoes, and greens of every kind as well as fragrant herbs and pungent garlic. Immersed in the abundance of field-fresh produce, Dave formed his culinary philosophy that food should be simple, not over-spiced, letting the flavors of the fresh produce combine to create the overall taste. Dave moved to McCall in the early 90s, working various jobs, including managing the produce department at a local grocery store. His love for food prompted him to get a job at a local restaurant, where he immersed himself in the intricacies of a commercial kitchen. This job led him to serve as Sous Chef for several area restaurants, which led him to follow his dream of owning his own restaurant.

A native Idahoan, Chef Sean Thueson grew up in the rural town of Jerome. He started working in restaurants during high school, working his way up through the ranks at a variety of venues. Working in Sun Valley, Boise, and Seattle, Sean learned the elements of a variety of cuisines including Mexican, German, and cross cultural fusion. While managing a seafood restaurant in Seattle, Sean received his certification as Chef de Cuisine. Wanting to return to Idaho, Sean accepted a position at Bear Creek Lodge, where Dave was serving as chef at the time. After working together, the two chefs realized that they had similar culinary philosophies and decided to venture out on their own with the Epicurean.

At the Epicurean, you will find a wide variety of gastronomic delights. Choose from an array of appetizers like Calamari with Lemon-Plum Sauce, or Coconut Crab Cakes with Roasted Tomatillo and Mango Salsa. Entrees include favorites like Seared Ahi Tuna on Wakame Seaweed Noodle Salad, Rack of Lamb with Hunan BBQ Sauce, and the award-winning Beef Wellington, rated Best of Beef by the Idaho Beef Council. But, be sure to save room for a luscious selection of homemade desserts including velvety Chocolate Mousse and Ginger Crème Brûlée with Mango Chop. You can also enjoy wine from the extensive wine list, featuring wines from the West Coast as well as Australia, Spain, and Italy.

# Raviolis with Lobster-Cognac Sage Sauce and Lobster Tails

## Ingredients

*6 4- to 6-ounce lobster tails*
*6 ounces mushrooms, sliced*
*3 tablespoons olive oil*
*Lobster-Cognac Sage Sauce (recipe follows)*
*2½ pounds cheese raviolis, cooked al dente and lightly oiled*

## Preparation

PREPARE the lobster tails by cutting lengthwise down the top of the shell with sharp kitchen scissors. Pry the shell apart and pull the tail meat out of the skeleton, leaving the end attached.

IN A large sauté pan or wide pot, preheat olive oil and add mushrooms and lobster tails so that the meat is pan-side down. When the mushrooms are starting to soften, add the Lobster-Cognac Sage Sauce and the raviolis. Bring the sauce to a boil, and then turn it off. Turn the lobster tails over, making sure the meat remains in the sauce, and steep until they are done. Serve the raviolis and sauce with a lobster tail on top of each plate.

***Serves 6***

*Wine suggestion: For a white, try a Chardonnay or Viognier or for a red, try a Malbec or Shiraz*

## For the Lobster-Cognac Sage Sauce

*½ pound butternut squash*
*1½ tablespoons lobster or shrimp base*
*1 tablespoon fish or clam base*
*½ tablespoon dry sage*
*1 tablespoon shallot, minced*
*1 tablespoon garlic, chopped*
*¼ cup cognac or brandy*
*1 cup hot water*
*1 teaspoon nutmeg*
*2½ cups heavy cream*

PEEL and seed the squash. Boil it until it is completely done. Drain squash and place in blender or food processor with all the other ingredients except the cream. Purée the mixture, adding the cream at the end. Keep warm for service.

***Yield: 5 cups***

# Seafood Sunsplash

*with Lemon-Coconut Rum Sauce and Coconut Rice Cakes*

## Ingredients

- *4 ounces mushrooms, sliced*
- *2 large roasted peppers, sliced*
- *1 pound 16/20 count prawns, peeled and deveined*
- *1 pound 10/20 count sea scallops*
- *1 pound green lip mussels*
- *2 tablespoons olive oil*
- *2 cups Lemon-Coconut Rum Sauce (recipe follows)*
- *Coconut Rice Cakes (recipe follows)*
- *egg roll wonton skins, cut in strips and fried*

## Preparation

PLACE olive oil in a large sauté pan or wide pot. Add mushrooms, peppers, prawns, scallops, and mussels and sauté on high for about 2 minutes. Add the 2 cups of Lemon-Coconut Rum Sauce, bring mixture to a boil and then turn off heat. Using tongs, continue turning the seafood until it finishes cooking. Discard any mussels that have not opened up.

SERVE around Coconut Rice Cakes and top with strips of fried wonton skins.

***Serves 4***

*Wine suggestion: a Chardonnay or a Pinot if you prefer red*

## For the Lemon-Coconut Rum Sauce

- *2 tablespoons rum syrup*
- *1 cup coconut cream*
- *1½ cups crushed pineapple*
- *2 teaspoons Oriental chili sauce*
- *1 cup heavy cream*
- *1 tablespoon soy sauce*
- *½ cup lemon juice*
- *1 teaspoon nutmeg*
- *1 tablespoon fresh ginger, chopped*
- *1 bunch cilantro, chopped*
- *2 tablespoons fresh basil, chopped*

THOROUGHLY combine all ingredients in a large container.

***Yield: 4½ cups***

### For the Coconut Rice Cakes

*1 cup white rice*
*2 cups water*
*¼ cup coconut cream*
*toasted coconut*

BOIL rice and water until rice is done and water absorbed. While rice is still hot, firmly pack it into a cake pan or high-sided container so that the rice is at least 3 inches deep. Press firmly. Pour coconut cream lightly across top. Spread evenly with a spatula and sprinkle with toasted coconut. The rice will absorb the coconut cream as it cools. Let rice cool completely for easier cutting. Using a cookie cutter or a soup can with both ends removed, cut the rice into cakes. Microwave the rice cakes when your are ready to serve.

# Duck Napolean

*with Polenta and Brown Butter Sauce*

This recipe is made with duck confit that can be found in specialty gourmet markets. If you do not have access to duck confit, you can make this with chicken, as we describe below.

## Ingredients

- *4 chicken legs & thighs*
- *2 cups water*
- *2 tablespoons chicken base*
- *2 tablespoons fresh garlic, chopped*
- *1 pinch basil*
- *1 pinch oregano*
- *1 pinch rosemary*
- *12 discs Polenta (recipes follows)*
- *Brown Butter Sauce (recipe follows)*

## Preparation

HEAT oven to 275 degrees. Place the chicken legs and thighs in a braising pot. Add water, chicken base, garlic, and herbs. Bring to a simmer, cover, and place in 275-degree oven for 1½ hours. You may occasionally have to add water. Cook for another 30 minutes with the lid off. Don't add any more water at this point. Chicken should be tender and ready to fall off the bone. Remove the chicken and let cool enough to handle and remove the meat from the bones. Keep meat warm until ready to serve.

TO SERVE, you will be stacking 3 discs of polenta and 2 portions of duck confit or chicken on top of each other. Since this is not a very stable tower, you will place it sort of on its side across the plate. Start with a disc to the left side of the plate, followed by a portion of meat placed partly on the disc and partly on the right side of the disc. This is followed by another disc placed partly on the meat and partly to the right of the meat. Place the final disc on top in the same manner. Drizzle the serving with Brown Butter Sauce. This dish is especially nice served with pea vines lightly sautéed with butter and a pinch of salt, pepper, and garlic.

***Serves 4***

*Wine suggestion: a Sauvignon Blanc or Pinot Gris is perfect, or if you prefer red, try a Syrah or Merlot*

## For the Polenta

- *4 cups water*
- *4 ounces butter*
- *1 cup half & half*
- *2 tablespoons chicken base*
- *2 tablespoons fresh garlic, minced*
- *2 teaspoons dry basil*
- *2 teaspoons dry thyme*
- *2 teaspoons rosemary leaf*
- *2 teaspoons oregano*
- *2 cups cornmeal*

IN A large pot, bring everything except the cornmeal to a boil. Slowly whisk in the cornmeal. Let the bubbly "goo" cook for another 30 seconds. Once the cornmeal is incorporated, pour into a 9x13-inch cake pan and let set up in the refrigerator.

ONCE cooled and set up, cut out discs with a round cookie cutter that is 2½ to 3 inches in diameter.

### For the Brown Butter Sauce

- *4 cups water*
- *¼ cup chicken base*
- *4 tablespoons cornstarch, dissolved in 4 tablespoons water*
- *½ pound butter*

BRING water and chicken base to a boil in a pot. Lightly thicken it by whisking in the cornstarch mixture. Set aside. In another pot, boil the butter rapidly until the solids separate and "burn" on the bottom of the pot. The butter will now have a caramel color.

REMOVE the pot from the heat. Using a long-handled whisk and a mitted hand (to avoid steam burns) slowly drizzle in the thickened stock while rapidly whisking the mixture. This will cause quite a reaction, so be cautious. If the mixture separates, just whisk it and it should come back together.

# Hunan Rack of Lamb

## Ingredients

*4 12- to 14-ounce lamb racks, frenched*
*Ginger-Beer Marinade (recipe follows)*
*Hunan BBQ Sauce (recipe follows)*
*sesame seeds for garnish*

## Preparation

MARINATE the racks of lamb for at least 4 hours in the Ginger-Beer Marinade.

HEAT oven to 500 degrees. Remove from marinade and place racks on a baking sheet. Roast in 500-degree oven for 15 minutes for medium rare to medium.

CUT each rack into double chops and place on service plate. Ladle Hunan BBQ Sauce over the chops and then sprinkle sesame seeds across them.

***Serves 4***

*Wine suggestion: a full-bodied Zinfandel, Cabernet Sauvignon, or Rhone-style red*

## For the Ginger-Beer Marinade

*1 bottle beer*
*12 ounces water*
*½ cup soy sauce*
*2 tablespoons powdered ginger*
*1 teaspoon salt*
*1 teaspoon black pepper*
*1 teaspoon garlic powder*

COMBINE all ingredients and whisk well.

## For the Hunan BBQ Sauce

*3½ cups tomato juice*
*1 bunch cilantro, chopper*
*⅛ cup lime juice*
*⅛ cup sherry*
*⅛ cup hoisin sauce*
*⅛ cup soy sauce*
*⅛ cup honey*
*2 tablespoons garlic, minced*
*2 tablespoons fresh ginger, minced*
*¼ cup Oriental chili sauce*
*2 teaspoons coriander*
*2 tablespoons sesame oil*
*¼ cup cornstarch, diluted with ¼ cup water*

PLACE all ingredients except the cornstarch mixture in a pot and bring to a boil. Thicken by whisking in the cornstarch mixture. Keep warm until service.

# Copper Canyon

113 13th Ave S
Nampa, ID
208-461-0887
Catering 208-899-2944

Monday 11:00am to 2:00pm
Tuesday - Friday 11:00am to 10:00pm
Saturday 5:00pm to 10:00pm

# *Copper Canyon*

## *Brian Inaba, Owner/Chef*
## *Deanna Shaver, Owner*

The small, friendly town of Nampa has a jewel of a restaurant in Brian Inaba's Copper Canyon. Brian's hospitality makes all his guests feel at home, as he wanders among the tables, greeting long-term fans and newcomers alike. A chef with experience working in such notable places as the Columbia Gorge Hotel and the Snoqualmie Falls Lodge, Brian opened the Copper Canyon in 1999, in a tiny little space on 12th Avenue, one block away from its present location.

His reputation for excellent food often made it hard to get a reservation on a weekend, and prompted Brian to move to larger quarters on 13th Avenue in the spring of 2004. The larger venue still maintains a warm, intimate atmosphere, with walls painted in burnt sienna and adorned with mirrors, paintings, and a beautiful stylized rubber tree plant. Copper Canyon has a philosophy of trying to provide local, fresh ingredients for dishes that are made from scratch. He likes to use local beef and he also flies in fresh seafood from the Northwest to provide daily specials that are outstanding. When wild salmon and halibut are in season, you will usually find mouth-watering creations on the menu. Chef Brian also has a magic way with duck, which is usually on the menu or is featured in a special presentation. The wine list features many of the local wineries that abound in southwestern Idaho, and you can also enjoy some northwest regional microbrews.

In recent years, the Copper Canyon has offered a catering service to the Nampa area that has been well received. They have successfully catered many private parties as well as special events, including the St. Chapelle Jazz Series that is held every summer at the winery that is west of Lake Lowell.

An evening at the Copper Canyon can be an enjoyable experience, either as an intimate dinner for two or a fun party as you meet many of your neighbors or make new friends.

# Pan Fried Oysters

*with Tartar Sauce and Cole Slaw*

## Ingredients

- 12 *large oysters, shucked*
- 1 *cup flour*
- 1 *teaspoon cayenne pepper*
- 2 *teaspoons paprika*
- ½ *teaspoon chili powder*
- 1 *pinch thyme, to taste*
- 1 *teaspoon salt*
- 3 *cups peanut oil*
- *Tartar Sauce (recipe follows)*
- *Cole Slaw (recipe follows)*

## Preparation

IN A large skillet, heat oil to 350 degrees. In a large bowl, mix all dry ingredients thoroughly. Toss oysters in this mixture and shake to discard excess flour. Place oysters in hot oil carefully, so as not to burn yourself. Cook until golden brown. Remove oysters from oil and place on plate covered with paper towels to drain off excess oil.

PLACE drained oysters on individual plates with cole slaw, and serve with tartar sauce.

***Serves 4***

## For the Tartar Sauce

- 1 *cup mayonnaise*
- 1 *tablespoon sweet relish*
- 1 *tablespoon onion, minced*
- ½ *teaspoon Worcestershire sauce*
- 2 *tablespoons lemon juice*
- ½ *tablespoon dill pickle, minced*
- *Tabasco, to taste*
- *salt and pepper to taste*

IN A small bowl, mix all ingredients. This can be made ahead, and lasts 3 to 4 days in the refrigerator.

## For the Cole Slaw

- ¼ *medium red onion, thinly sliced*
- ½ *head Napa cabbage or head cabbage, finely sliced*
- 3 *green onions, sliced*
- ½ *teaspoon lemon juice*
- ¼ *cup mayonnaise*
- 3 *tablespoons soy sauce*
- 2 *tablespoons Dijon mustard*
- ½ *teaspoon sugar, optional*

MIX all ingredients in large bowl, adding sugar to taste if you like your cole slaw sweet. Refrigerate until ready to serve.

# Black Pepper Crusted Beef Tenderloin

*with Mushroom Ragout*

## Ingredients

- *4 6-ounce beef tenderloins, 1-inch thick*
- *1 teaspoon sugar*
- *2 tablespoons soy sauce*
- *2 tablespoons dry sherry*
- *1 teaspoon garlic, chopped*
- *¼ cup cracked black pepper*
- *vegetable oil*
- *Wild Mushroom Ragout (recipe follows)*

## Preparation

MIX sugar, soy sauce, sherry, and garlic together. Marinate steaks in this mixture for at least 1 hour. Lift steaks from marinade and sprinkle with cracked pepper on all sides, patting to make pepper stick.

HEAT oven to 125 degrees. Place a small amount of vegetable oil in a heavy-bottomed skillet and heat to smoking point. Put the steaks in the pan carefully, so as not you burn yourself. Cook 3 - 4 minutes per side for medium rare to medium. Remove from pan and place in warm oven until ready to serve.

***Serves 4***

## For the Wild Mushroom Ragout

- *1 pound assorted domestic and wild mushrooms*
- *1 tablespoon olive oil*
- *3 tablespoons shallots, chopped*
- *1 teaspoon garlic, chopped*
- *2 teaspoons fresh thyme, chopped*
- *2 tablespoons Marsala wine*
- *1 cup beef stock*
- *1 teaspoon lemon juice*
- *¼ cup heavy cream, optional*
- *salt and pepper to taste*

HEAT oil in large sauté pan over medium high heat. Add mushrooms and cook for 2 minutes. Stir in shallots, garlic, and thyme. Add Marsala wine and stock and reduce until thick. Add lemon juice and adjust seasoning with salt and pepper. If a richer sauce is desired, add heavy cream and heat to warm.

# *Andrae's*

816 West Bannock
Boise, ID 83702
208-385-0707
www.andraesboise.com

**Dinner**
Monday – Wednesday 5:30pm to close
Thursday –Saturday 5:00pm to close
Reservations recommended

# *Andrae's*

## *Andrae and Michelle Bopp, Owners*

In late 2004, Andrae's opened its doors in downtown Boise, and foodies from all over Idaho rejoiced. Located on the 8th Street Market Corridor, Chef Andrae Bopp and his wife Michelle finally brought big-city contemporary French cuisine to this burgeoning tech-driven town. They put Boise on a map of Northwest dining destinations that includes Portland, San Francisco, and Seattle.

Bopp trained at the French Culinary Institute and worked at Le Bernardin in New York City. This training is put to good use at Andrae's. A meal at this warmly intimate restaurant starts with a gratis flute of champagne and an amuse to set the taste buds awhirl. Depending on the chef's whim, the amuse could be a crispy tiny Parmesan tuile filled with prosciutto di Parma ice cream or a fresh Florida rock shrimp, crusted in phyllo dough and rosemary and flash fried. From there, you settle into your cozy private booth to ponder the award-winning wine list that features one of the Northwest's best French and regional selections. Andrae's has seasonal prix fixe or tasting menus. There is also a chef's table available in the intimate wine cellar.

Seafood reigns supreme at Andrae's. Bopp has it flown in three times a week from a supplier in Maine, and his choices are always adventurous. His dishes feature the freshest seafood available presented with remarkable flair. Bopp uses locally grown organic produce and regional organic meats. A typical meal might start with Taylor Bay scallop ravioli filled with kumquat confit, American spoonbill caviar, and a serving of Yuzu soy vinaigrette. Entrée choice may be rosefish ala Bocusé with hand-turned vegetables or a roasted New England monkfish on braised red cabbage with a smoky bacon and black pepper sauce. Meat lovers gravitate to the braised Niman Ranch prime short ribs in port-infused veal demi-glace with warm purple fingerling potato salad or the sous Vide guinea hen with braised Oregon morels and prosciutto-wrapped white asparagus.

Desserts have equal footing at Andrae's. Whether you end with the warm Valrhona chocolate brioche pudding, buttermilk panna cotta with vanilla grapefruit sauce or the decadently rich crème brulée ice cream, you'll never forget dinner at Andrae's.

Award of Excellence

# Porcini Velouté with Scallops

## Ingredients

*5 tablespoons butter, divided*
*1 onion, peeled & rough chopped*
*8 ounces whole porcini mushrooms*
*3 cups cream*
*5 cups chicken stock*
*16 porcini mushrooms, halved*
*8 scallops*
*salt & pepper to taste*
*thyme leaves, for garnish*

## Preparation

TO MAKE the velouté, heat 3 tablespoons of the butter in a sauté pan. Add onion and sweat for 5 minutes. Add 8 ounces of porcini mushrooms and cook for 5 minutes, season with salt and pepper. Add cream and simmer for 10 minutes. Add stock and simmer for 10 minutes. Transfer to a blender and purée until smooth. Strain through a fine sieve and season with salt and pepper to taste. Set aside and keep warm.

ADD remaining butter to a sauté pan. Season scallops with salt, and add scallops and halved porcini mushrooms to pan, sautéing until golden brown. Remove and quarter the scallops.

TO SERVE, ladle velouté into bowl, top with scallops and porcinis, and then garnish with thyme leaves.

***Serves 8***

*Wine suggestion: Pouilly-Fumé De Ladoucette, 2002*

# Creamed Watercress

## Ingredients

*2 bunches watercress*
*3 tablespoons butter*
*1 cup heavy cream*
*salt*
*white pepper*

## Preparation

WASH and stem the watercress, and rough chop the leaves. Melt the butter and cook the leaves until wilted. Add the cream and boil for 2 minutes. Purée in a blender and season to taste.

***Serves 2***

*Wine suggestion: Boty Sémillon/Sauvignon Blanc 2003*

# Foie Gras Chestnut and Apple Stuffing

## Ingredients

*2 pounds fresh foie gras*
*4 cups brioche, cubed*
*butter, as needed*
*1 cup cippolini onions, peeled & quartered*
*6 Fuji apples, peeled, cored, & quartered*
*2 cups chestnuts, roasted, peeled, & quartered*
*1 cup seedless red grapes*
*4 cups arugula, stemmed*
*4 tablespoons parsley, chopped*
*2 tablespoons sage, chopped*
*salt & pepper*
*¾ cup chicken stock*

## Preparation

HEAT oven to 375 degrees. Cube the foie gras and refrigerate. Sauté the brioche in the butter until browned, and then cool. Heat a sauté pan over high heat and get smoking hot. Season the foie and sear until dark golden brown. Drain off and reserve the foie, adding the fat back into the pan and bring heat back up.

CUT each apple quarter into 3 even pieces. Add the onions, apples, and chestnuts to the heated pan and sauté until the mixture is golden brown. Season the mixture and remove to a bowl. Place the grapes and arugula in the pan and wilt the arugula in some of the fat; remove and add to the apple mixture. Add the foie and the brioche to the apples and mix well. Season and add the chopped herbs and chicken stock. Spread the stuffing evenly in a nonstick 2-inch pan. Bake for 20 minutes, until the top becomes crisp.

***Serves 12 – 14***

*Wine suggestion: Beaune Cle des Mouches, Joseph Brouhin, 2003*

# Guinea Hen Coq au Vin

## Ingredients

*5 ounces smoked bacon, cut into strips*
*1 6-pound guinea hen, cut into 6 – 8 pieces*
*salt & pepper*
*8 ounces flour*
*1 carrot, rough chopped*
*1 onion, rough chopped*
*3 cups red Burgundy*
*½ cup brandy*
*Bouquet Garni (thyme/rosemary sprig, garlic clove, peppercorns, parsley stems)*
*8 ounces baby chanterelles or larger, cut into small pieces*
*8 tablespoons butter, divided*
*8 ounces white pearl onions*
*brioche slices, cut into diamonds*
*clarified butter*
*chopped parsley*
*1–2 tablespoons Cognac or good vinegar, to finish*

## Preparation

SAUTÉ the bacon slowly to release all of the fat. Remove the bacon pieces and reserve. Season the hen in salt and pepper and dredge in flour. Brown the chopped carrot and onion in the bacon fat. Remove vegetables; add the hen and brown on all sides. Remove the browned hen and discard the fat. Put the cooked vegetables, hen, red wine, brandy, and Bouquet Garni in a pot. Cover and simmer for 1½ hours on the stovetop, or in the oven at 325 degrees. When the hen is done, the meat should be falling off the bone.

SAUTÉ the mushrooms in 4 tablespoons of the butter until lightly browned and set aside. Cook the pearl onions until soft, set aside. Lightly brown the croutons in the clarified butter.

CAREFULLY remove the hen from the pot and strain the liquid into a saucepot. Reduce liquid until you have a deep flavor. Add the rest of the butter, 1 tablespoon at a time, until desired consistency is achieved. For additional flavor, add 1-2 tablespoons of Cognac or good vinegar at the finish. Reheat the hen and vegetables in the sauce.

SERVE with the croutons that have had 1 tip dipped in the sauce and then in the parsley.

***Serves 6***

*Wine suggestion: Pommard. Les Grand Epenots V.V., Vincent Girardin, 2003*

# Venison Rack with Venison Sauce

The richly flavored Venison Sauce will take about an hour and a half to prepare, so trim the venison rack early and prepare the sauce through the reduction of the stock. Do not add the butter to the sauce until you are ready to serve the rack.

## Ingredients

*1 venison rack, trimmed, frenched & tied*
*2 tablespoons canola oil*
*salt & pepper to taste*
*Venison Sauce (recipe follows)*

## Preparation

HEAT oven to 450 degrees. Allow venison to sit at room temp for about 15 minutes prior to cooking. Season the rack with salt and pepper. In a skillet, heat canola oil over high heat. Brown the venison by searing it for 2-3 minutes on each side. Transfer to a large roasting pan and roast for about 8 minutes in 450-degree oven. Turn the rack over and roast for 7 more minutes for medium rare. Remove and transfer to a platter, cover and let rest for 10 minutes.

CARVE into single or double chops, depending on the course. Ladle Venison Sauce onto plates and place chops over sauce.

***Serves 4***

## For the Venison Sauce

*trimmings from 1 venison rack*
*1 tablespoon canola oil*
*2 shallots, peeled and sliced*
*2 garlic cloves, peeled and sliced*
*2 teaspoons black peppercorns*
*1 tablespoon juniper berries*
*1 thyme sprig*
*1 cup red wine*
*1½ quarts chicken stock*
*salt & pepper to taste*
*¼ cup butter*

HEAT the oil in a saucepan, and brown the trimmings for about 10 minutes. Transfer to a bowl and set aside. Add the shallots to the pan and cook, stirring for about 5 minutes. Add the garlic, peppercorns, juniper berries, and thyme, and cook for about 2 minutes. Return the browned trimmings to the pan and add the wine. Bring to a boil over high heat and boil for 10-15 minutes, until reduced to ¼ cup. Add the stock, reduce the heat to low and simmer for 1 hour. Stock should be reduced to 1 quart. Strain through a fine sieve, and discard solids. Return strained sauce to pan, skim off fat, and simmer over medium heat until reduced to about 1½ cups. Season to taste with salt and pepper and keep warm until ready to serve.

AT SERVICE, swirl in butter to enrich the sauce.

***Yield: approximately 1½ cups***

*Wine suggestion: Basel Cellars Syrah, 2002*

# Mourvèdre Sorbet

## Ingredients

*½ cup mourvèdre or light rose wine*

*1 cup Simple Syrup (recipe follows)*

COMBINE both ingredients and freeze according to your ice cream freezer's instructions. This will be a little soft, so place in freezer to firm up before serving.

***Serves 6***

## For the Simple Syrup

COMBINE equal parts sugar and water in a saucepan and bring to a simmer until all of the sugar is dissolved. Cool before using.

# Angell's Bar & Grill

999 West Main
Boise, ID 83702
208-342-4900
www.angellsbarandgrill.com

Lunch
Tuesday - Friday from 11:30 am
Dinner
Monday - Sunday from 5:00pm

# Angell's Bar & Grill

### Curt Knipe, Owner

With over a quarter of a century of serving Boise locals and visitors, Angell's Bar and Grill is one of the older dining establishments in the area. It wears its reputation well, serving fresh and fabulous meals in a relaxed and casual atmosphere.

Stepping down from street level at the corner of Main and 9th, you enter Angell's through the beautiful outdoor patio featuring a two-tiered deck, fountains, gazebos, and an abundance of natural foliage and colorful hanging baskets. This is a perfect place to enjoy a lunch on a sunny afternoon or a romantic dinner on a warm Boise summer evening. But you will also delight in the comfort of the interior dining room. A lodge-like ambience has been created with a décor that features rich hunter-green wainscoting, plush leather armchairs, and high-backed leather upholstered booths, softly lit by copper ceiling lamps. African wildlife trophies and pictures adorn the walls along with game fish trophies and beautiful examples of Idaho wildfowl.

Over the restaurant's history, Owner Curt Knipe has learned how to read his customers and to put the knowledge to work in creating his ever-evolving successful menu items. On recent menus you could try as appetizers, Baked Raspberry Brie served with raspberries and sauce served with toasted baguette points or Blue Crab & Artichoke Hearts baked with diced onions, herbs and seasoned aioli, served with toast points. The Cantonese Chicken Salad has been a favorite on their menu for a long time, as the locals constantly request it. For entrées, try the Black& Bleu Lamb Chops that have been crusted with Cajun seasoning, charbroiled and served with bleu cheese and vegetable relish. Or enjoy the Raspberry Balsamic Pork Rack, a hand cut pork rack that has been char grilled, basted with garlic butter, and glazed with a raspberry balsamic reduction. And, if fish is your forte, Angell's serves a selection of fresh Northwest fish, including Alaskan halibut, Artic char, and Pacific salmòn as well as Idaho trout and Pacific ahi tuna.

To accompany your culinary experience, Angell's Bar & Grill offers a full bar featuring hand-shaken martinis and house specials. With over 85 wines in their cellar, you can be assured that you will be able to find the perfect wines to pair with our dining choices. Angell's Bar & Grill has been a winner of the Northwest Cuisine Award every year since its opening in 1981, proving that the restaurant's quality of service and culinary ability has been maintained over the years.

# Cantonese Chicken Salad with Curry Dressing

This tangy and crunchy salad is one of our most requested recipes.

## Ingredients

- 2 *medium heads iceberg lettuce, shredded*
- 1 *cup celery, chopped*
- ¼ *cup cilantro, chopped*
- 1¾ *cups chow mein noodles*
- ¼ *cup vegetable oil*
- 1¾ *pounds boneless chicken breasts, skinned & sliced into 2-inch pieces*
- 12 *ounces sliced water chestnuts, drained*
- 1¾ *cups snow peas, cut diagonally into 3 pieces*
- 2¾ *cups Curry Dressing, divided (recipe follows)*
- ¼ *cup sliced almonds*
- 10 *radishes, thinly sliced*
- 2 *green onions, finely chopped*

## Preparation

COMBINE lettuce, celery, and cilantro in a glass salad bowl. Spread noodles over mixture. Heat oil in large, heavy skillet over medium-high heat. Add chicken and stir until lightly browned, about 2 minutes. Add water chestnuts and snow peas and continue cooking while stirring for about 1 minute. Remove mixture from skillet using a slotted spoon, and arrange over salad.

ADD 2 cups of the Curry Dressing and toss to combine. Garnish with almonds, radishes, and green onions and serve. Pass the remaining dressing separately.

***Serves 6 – 8***

## For the Curry Dressing

- 3 *tablespoons dry white wine*
- 2 *tablespoons unsweetened pineapple juice*
- 2 *tablespoons fresh lemon juice*
- 2 *tablespoons light brown sugar, firmly packed*
- 1½ *tablespoons curry powder*
- 2 *teaspoons soy sauce*
- 1 *teaspoons onion powder*
- 1 *pinch garlic powder*
- 2 *cups mayonnaise*

COMBINE all ingredients, except the mayonnaise, in a non-reactive bowl. Stir until the brown sugar has completely dissolved. Add the mayonnaise several spoonfuls at a time, blending until the dressing is smooth.

***Yield: 2¾ cups***

# Juniper Rosemary Lamb Rack

## Ingredients

- ¼ *cup juniper berries*
- 2 *sprigs fresh rosemary, stripped*
- 1 *tablespoon garlic, rough chopped*
- ½ *cup olive oil*
- 1 *7-8 ounce rack of lamb, frenched*
- 2 *ounces apple mint jelly*
- 7 *ounces fresh apple chutney*

## Preparation

PLACE juniper berries, rosemary, and garlic in a food processor and blend. Slowly add olive oil until a paste is formed. Rub paste on the rack of lamb, and let it rest for about 1 hour.

HEAT grill and cook rack of lamb until it reaches an internal temperature of 135°. Mix apple mint jelly and apple chutney together. To serve, place rack on a platter and serve the chutney mixture on the side or on top of the rack.

***Serves 1***

*Downtown Boise.*

# Asiago's

asiago's

Asiago's Ristorante
3423 N. Cole Road
Boise, ID 83702
208-323-1469
Monday - Friday 11:30am to Close
Saturday - Sunday 4:00pm to Close

Asiago's Downtown
1002 Main Street
Boise, ID 83704
208-336-5552
www.asiagos.com
Monday - Friday 11:00am to Close
Saturday - Sunday 4:00pm to Close

# *Asiago's*

## *Jason Driver, Owner*
## *David Knickrehm, CEC, Executive Chef*

Asiago's Ristorante opened in the fall of 1997. Jason Driver, a founding owner of Asiago's, drew on his Napa Valley restaurant experience when conceiving his new restaurant's menu and wine list. The Ristorante is decidedly upscale but unstuffy, and guests can enjoy the fresh flavors of Italy and California wine country. Beginning with pasta made in-house daily, the menu is prepared from scratch in the exhibition kitchen, and features seasonal specials, salads, sandwiches, soups, and desserts. The setting is vineyard-rustic with handmade tables, fieldstone and stucco walls, and a rugged wood pergola twined with grapevines standing over all. The unpretentious setting allows you to relax and enjoy the culinary experience with the help of a well-trained staff intent on making your visit a memorable one. The wine bar features an extensive list of wines from California, Italy, New Zealand, and the Northwest, as well as a large selection of draft microbrews.

Opened in 2002, Asiago's Downtown continued on the original theme established by the Ristorante. The smaller size of the downtown location lends a special intimacy to the place. The dining area surrounds you with the turn of the century brick walls, imported Italian tiling on the floors, stained glass windows, and white lights strung form the vaulted ceiling, imparting a sense of an old Italian street café. The large front glass windows overlook Main Street as well as patio seating surrounded by terra cotta planters. During the warmer months, this area provides comfortable seating in the open air for both lunch and dinner. The menu at this location, although not an exact duplicate, mirrors the Ristorante's culinary vision, and the wine list also features many of the same wines from California, Italy, New Zealand, and the Northwest.

Both restaurants are under the watchful eye of Executive Chef David Knickrehm. He is a graduate of Le Cordon Bleu in Ottawa, Canada, where he received culinary training in European and Mediterranean cuisines. Chef Knickrehm also has culinary expertise in Chinese, Japanese, and Vietnamese cuisines. In 2004 he achieved the prestigious Certified Executive Chef (C.E.C.) certification from the American Culinary Federation.

His expertise has helped win Asiago's many local awards for outstanding restaurant, chief among them being the *Idaho Statesman's* "Best of the Treasure Valley" award for 2005 and the *Boise Weekly's* "Best of Boise 2005" award.

# Bruschetta Pomodoro

This recipe is a guaranteed hit. You might want to practice the bread recipe if you are unfamiliar with making fresh bread. The Pomodoro also works well with crusty bread available at a bakery or grocery store. You will also have better results if you refrigerate the tomato/basil combination overnight.

## Ingredients

- 1 *quart tomatoes, seeded & diced*
- ¼ *cup fresh basil, chiffonade*
- 1 *teaspoon kosher salt*
- 1 *teaspoon fine black pepper*
- 1 *tablespoon garlic, minced*
- 1 *teaspoon balsamic vinegar*
- ½ *teaspoon brown sugar*
- 1 *ounce white sugar*
- 1½ *cups water, heated to 110°*
- ¼ *ounce yeast*
- 2 *pounds bread flour*
- ½ *ounce ground rosemary*
- ½ *ounce kosher salt*
- *extra virgin olive oil*

## Preparation

FOR chiffonade, roll basil leaves into cylinders and chop into thin strips. In a non-reactive bowl, combine the basil, tomatoes, salt, pepper, garlic, vinegar, and brown sugar. Gently toss and refrigerate overnight, allowing flavors to meld.

TO MAKE the bread, dissolve sugar in the heated water. Sprinkle yeast into mixture and allow to stand until foamy. Mix flour and rosemary in a large mixing bowl. Form a well in the center and mix in yeast mixture. Knead together 20 minutes. Add salt and knead an additional 10 minutes. Cover and allow to rise at room temperature for 1 hour. Punch down dough and cover again, allowing to rise 45 minutes.

HEAT oven to 350 degrees. Form dough into two long baguette shapes and bake at 350 degrees for 12-15 minutes, or until internal temperature reaches 190°. Cool on wire rack.

AT TIME of service slice the cooled baguettes in half, brush with olive oil and grill. Serve grilled rosemary bread with tomato mixture.

***Serves 8***

*Wine suggestion: A Chardonnay with balanced fruit and toasty oak character, or a Napa Valley Pinot Grigio pairs nicely with the bruschetta.*

# PANZANELLA

*with Balsamic Vinaigrette*

This recipe follows the Tuscan principal of complete utilization. Yesterday's bread becomes today's soup or salad.

## Ingredients

*1 large head green leaf lettuce*
*1 pound stale bread*
*1 red bell pepper*
*1 green bell pepper*
*Balsamic Vinaigrette (recipe follows)*
*2 tomatoes, diced*
*2 cups Asiago cheese, grated*

## Preparation

WASH lettuce and shake dry. Chop lettuce and place in large salad bowl. Tear bread into bite-size pieces and add to salad. Julienne peppers, discarding seeds and veins. Add Balsamic Vinaigrette and diced tomatoes, toss, and serve topped with Asiago cheese.

***Serves 4***

*Wine suggestion: This salad pairs well with a dry German Riesling or a fruit-forward red table wine.*

## For the Balsamic Vinaigrette

*2 tablespoons brown sugar*
*⅓ cup balsamic vinegar*
*2 egg yolks*
*1 teaspoon garlic, minced*
*½ teaspoon dry basil leaves*
*1 teaspoon kosher salt*
*½ teaspoon fine grind black pepper*
*1 cup salad oil*

COMBINE brown sugar, balsamic vinegar, egg yolks, minced garlic, basil, kosher salt, and pepper in a food processor. Drizzle oil into running food processor in a slow steady stream. Refrigerate balsamic vinaigrette immediately.

***Yield: approximately 1½ cups***

# Funghi Prosecco

The technique for "mounting" a sauce with butter is one of a chef's most important secrets. Swirling the cold butter into a reduction both thickens and enriches a sauce. Care must be taken to keep the pan moving, or the butter will separate and the sauce will "break".

## Ingredients

- *32 medium button mushrooms*
- *½ cup olive oil*
- *2 tablespoons garlic, minced*
- *1 cup Prosecco (Champagne or sparkling wine)*
- *salt and pepper*
- *1 teaspoon parsley, minced*
- *½ teaspoon lemon zest, minced*
- *½ stick cold butter, cubed*

## Preparation

SHAKE mushrooms in a dry towel to dislodge any residual dirt. Heat oil in large sauté pan. Sauté mushrooms over medium heat approximately 5 minutes. Add garlic and sauté until fragrant, but do not brown. De-glaze pan with Prosecco and season to taste. Add parsley and lemon zest and reduce until very little liquid remains. Remove pan from heat and swirl in cold butter. Continue to swirl pan until all the butter is incorporated and sauce is thick and glossy.

***Serves 4***

*Wine suggestion: A full-bodied, slightly oaky Pinot Gris is an excellent choice with this dish.*

# Vitello Caprese

This simple preparation has become one of our signature dishes. Its flavors are bright and straightforward. The balsamic vinegar reduction is prepared the day before serving.

## Ingredients

*1 cup balsamic vinegar*
*1 pound linguine*
*olive oil for pasta*
*12 2-ounce veal scaloppini*
*salt and pepper*
*1 cup flour*
*¼ cup olive oil*
*12 slices vine ripe tomatoes*
*16 large basil leaves, divided*
*12 1-ounce slices buffalo mozzarella*
*⅓ cup butter*
*1 tablespoon parsley, minced*
*1 teaspoon lemon zest, minced*

## Preparation

THE day before, simmer the balsamic vinegar until it is reduced to 1/3 cup. Cool and place in a plastic squeeze bottle.

COOK dry linguine in 1 gallon of boiling salted water. When cooked to desired doneness, drain and plunge into cold water. Drain pasta a second time and lightly oil, reserving for service.

HEAT oven to 400 degrees. Season veal with salt and pepper and dredge each scaloppini in flour. Heat olive oil in a large sauté pan and sauté each scaloppini 1 minute on each side. Transfer veal to a sheet pan and top with 1 tomato slice, 1 basil leaf, and 1 buffalo mozzarella slice, respectively. Finish veal in the oven for 5 minutes or until cheese has just begun to melt.

WHILE veal is in the oven, heat butter in large sauté pan. Allow butter to cook until it turns nut brown. Immediately remove from heat and cool for 1 minute. Add parsley, lemon zest, and linguine and toss to coat.

USING tongs, divide pasta and place on 4 plates. Surround each mound of pasta with 3 veal medallions. Drizzle reduced balsamic vinegar around tips of veal and garnish pasta with a fresh basil leaf.

***Serves 4***

*Wine suggestion: This pairs nicely with a full-bodied Pinot Noir or a fruity Shiraz.*

# Carne Selvaggio Caccciatore

At the restaurant we serve this dish with Dijon-flavored mashed potatoes and buttered asparagus. A note on the demi-glace: This is a double strength veal stock thickened with roux. Gourmet stores carry concentrated or powdered demi-glace. Due to the complex flavors in this dish 'brown gravy' can be substituted with some degree of success.

## Ingredients

*4 8-ounce elk sirloin steaks (venison can be substituted)*
*salt and pepper to taste*
*2 tablespoons olive oil*
*1 cup button mushrooms, quartered*
*1 cup tomatoes, diced*
*2 shallots, minced*
*½ cup cooked bacon bits*
*2 tablespoons green peppercorns*
*¼ cup red currant jelly*
*⅓ cup white wine*
*½ cup demi-glace (see note above)*
*¼ cup green onions, chopped*
*½ stick cold butter, cubed*

## Preparation

HEAT oven to 375 degrees. Season steaks liberally with salt and pepper. Heat oil in large sauté pan and sear steaks on each side. Remove steaks to a sheet pan and place in oven 10 minutes for medium rare.

IN THE original sauté pan add mushrooms, tomatoes, shallots, bacon bits, green peppercorns, and red currant jelly. Sauté together 3 minutes. De-glaze pan with wine. When just a little liquid remains add demi-glace. When sauce begins to thicken, remove from heat and add green onions. Remove pan from heat and swirl cold butter into sauce to add richness and shine. Remove steaks from oven and serve crowned with sauce.

***Serves 4***

*Wine suggestion: Fine wines to compliment this complex dish would be a bold Petite Syrah or California Cabernet.*

*Pierce Park in Boise ca. 1910*

# Bar Gernika

Gernika Basque Pub & Eatery
202 S Capitol Blvd
Boise, ID 83702
208-344-2175
Monday – Saturday
11:00am to 11:00pm

The Basque Market
608 W. Grove Street
Boise, ID 83702
208-433-1208
www.thebasquemarket.com
Monday – Saturday
10:00am to 6:30pm

# Gernika Basque Pub & Eatery

### *Dan Ansotegui, Owner*

Also known as Bar Gernika, this friendly tavern and restaurant anchors the western end of the Basque Block, which runs along Grove Street from S. Capitol Boulevard to S. 6th Street. A member of a prominent Basque family, Dan Ansotegui took his first trip to Basque Country in 1978, where he began to envision a small restaurant serving Basque fare along the lines of lighter sandwiches and tapas. In June 1991 he opened Bar Gernika in the lovely old building that was originally built in 1920 as a Chinese laundry. At that time, Boise's Chinatown and the Basque area crisscrossed right at this intersection. Solomo and Chorizo sandwiches were served at the restaurant from its first day. Over the years, the menu has increased to include, lamb, a simple paella, homemade soups, and fresh salads.

Dan began to do a lot of catering, including fundraising for local schools, but the catering soon became too much for the small pub to handle. At the same time, more Spanish and Basque products were coming into the Boise market, as Basque food became increasingly popular. In December 2000, Dan opened The Basque Market in the center of the Basque Block. This little gem of a store carries the largest selection of Spanish and Basque wines in Idaho, as well as olives, peppers, spices, rice, beans, sausages, chocolates, and cookies.

The store not only does the catering, but also is set up for cooking classes that feature Basque specialties. The full commercial kitchen is very open and cooking classes/wine tastings are held twice a month. A private class for groups of 12 or more can also be arranged, which turns out to be a fun party. Stop in and talk to Dan about catering an outdoor paella party for groups from 20 to 200. This is a special experience, as Dan and his crew bring giant paella pans to your location. The cooking of paella is quite an art, and Dan is ready to share the history of the dish as well as the technique of making it with you and your guests.

A trip to the Basque Block is a special experience that you will not want to miss. Stroll the block and enjoy the Basque Cultural Center and Museum, and tour the historic Cyrus Jacobs/Uberuaga House. Originally built in 1864 by Cyrus Jacobs as his residence, the house became a Basque boarding house in 1910 and was home to many Basques who came to Idaho in the early 20th century. Then, you can finish with a shopping trip to The Basque Market and a fine Basque meal at Bar Gernika.

# Shrimp Stuffed Piquillo Peppers

*with Pimiento Sauce*

## Ingredients

- *2 tablespoons butter*
- *¼ cup olive oil*
- *¼ cup onion, chopped*
- *1 pound shrimp, peeled and deveined*
- *¾ cup flour*
- *3 cups milk*
- *⅛ cup parsley, chopped*
- *salt to taste*
- *1 can piquillo peppers*
- *Pimiento Sauce (recipe follows)*

## Preparation

IN A heavy-bottomed pan melt butter with the olive oil. Sauté onion at low heat until translucent. Add shrimp and continue cooking until shrimp just turns pink. Remove pan from heat and shrimp from pan. Chop shrimp into small pieces. Return pan to heat and add shrimp. Add flour to make a heavy roux. Slowly add milk, mixing thoroughly with the flour to make a smooth mixture. Add parsley and salt to taste. Set aside to cool.

HEAT oven to 425 degrees. Fill piquillo peppers with cooled shrimp mixture, using a pastry bag or a zip lock bag with the corner cut off. Place on sheet pan and put in 425-degree oven for about 12 to 15 minutes. Top with Pimiento Sauce.

***Serves 6 - 8 as an appetizer***

*Wine suggestions: Izadi White Viuda, El Coto Crianza, or El Coto reserva*

## For the Pimiento Sauce

- *2 tablespoons olive oil*
- *4 garlic cloves, sliced thin*
- *7 piquillo peppers*
- *¼ cup white wine*
- *1 7-ounce can tomato sauce*
- *salt to taste*

HEAT oil in a small skillet and sauté the garlic. Add peppers and continue to sauté for another 5-7 minutes. Add wine, tomato sauce, and about 1 teaspoon salt. Simmer for 5 minutes. Remove from heat and blend with a food processor until it reaches a smooth consistency. Use right away or store in refrigerator and reheat when needed.

# Basque Red Bean Soup

To achieve a really flavorful soup, be sure to use a quality beef base that has beef as the first ingredient.

## Ingredients

- *1 pound small red beans*
- *1 gallon cold water*
- *¾ cup olive oil, divided*
- *1 large leek, diced*
- *1 green pepper, diced*
- *¼ cup beef base*
- *½ onion, finely chopped*
- *1 14-ounce can tomato sauce*

## Preparation

RINSE beans in cold water. Place beans and water in a large stockpot at medium high heat. Add ½ cup of the olive oil, reserving the rest for later. Add leek and green pepper and cook at a slow boil for 2 hours. Add beef base and continue simmering another hour, or until broth has thickened and the beans are tender to taste. Sauté the onion in the remaining olive oil until softened. Add to the soup along with the tomato sauce. Add salt to taste, heat through, and serve.

***Serves about 12***

# The Basque Market's Chorizo, Chicken & Pork Paella

If you have leftover cooked chicken or pork, they can also be used in this dish.

## Ingredients

*6 cups chicken broth*
*12 strands saffron*
*2 tablespoons olive oil*
*½ pound chicken meat, cut up*
*½ pound pork loin, cut up*
*½ onion, diced*
*2-3 garlic cloves, chopped*
*½ green pepper, diced*
*2 chorizo sausages, cup up*
*¼ pound jamon Serrano, diced – or substitute prosciutto*
*2 linguica sausages, cut up*
*2 cups medium rice*
*½ cup pimientos, diced*
*½ cup frozen peas and carrots*

## Preparation

BRING broth with the saffron threads to a low simmer on a back burner. You will be adding this in batches.

IN A paella pan for 8 people add the oil and place on medium-low heat. If chicken and pork are uncooked, sauté them until they are about two-thirds done. Remove and set aside. Sauté the onion until it is translucent, about 10 minutes. Add garlic and cook until the aroma is noticeable. Add green pepper and cook for about 5 minutes, being careful not to let vegetables brown. Add chorizo, jamon Serrano, and linguica, cooking until they are nearly cooked through. Return chicken and pork to pan and add rice and pimientos, stirring well. Add three-quarters of the broth, leaving the rest to simmer. Mix everything well so that the rice is at an even depth throughout the pan. Do not stir the rice from this point on. Add about one-half of the remaining broth. Add peas and carrots and more broth, if necessary. You will probably use all but about ½ cup of broth, but you may need it all. Continue cooking until rice is done. Remove from heat and allow to rest for about 10 minutes before serving.

***Serves 8 – 10***

*Wine suggestion: For a red, Luis Alegre Crianza from Rioja, and for a white, Ermita Veracruz verdejo 2004*

# The Basque Market's Mixed Paella

## Ingredients

- 6 *cups chicken broth*
- 12 *strands saffron*
- 2 *tablespoons olive oil*
- ½ *pound chicken meat, cut in 1-inch cubes*
- ½ *onion, diced*
- 2-3 *garlic cloves, chopped*
- ½ *green pepper, diced*
- 2 *chorizo sausages, cut up*
- 2 *cups medium rice*
- ½ *cup pimientos, diced*
- ½ *cup frozen peas and carrots*
- 1 *pound clams or cockles*
- ½ *pound mussels*
- ¾ *pound shrimp, peeled and deveined*

## Preparation

HEAT the broth with the saffron threads on a back burner to a low simmer. You will be adding the broth to the paella in batches.

IN A paella pan for 8 people (34cm) add the oil on medium-low heat. Sauté the chicken until it is about two-thirds done. Remove the chicken and set aside. Sauté the onion until it is translucent, about 10 minutes. Add garlic and cook until the aroma becomes noticeable. Add green pepper and sauté about 5 minutes, being careful to keep the vegetables from browning. Add chorizo and cook until nearly cooked through. Return chicken to pan and add rice, stirring well. Add about one-half to two-thirds of the broth, leaving the rest to simmer. Add pimientos and the peas and carrots, mixing well so that the rice is spread evenly throughout the pan. Add clams, mussels, and shrimp so that they are dispersed evenly. Do not stir the rice from this point. Add about one-half of the remaining broth. You will probably use all but ½ cup of the broth. If some of the mussels or clams do not open, exchange them with opened ones in hotter parts of the pan or put them in the remaining simmering broth to open. Continue cooking until the rice is done. Remove from heat and allow to rest for about 10 minutes before serving.

***Serves 8 – 10***

*Wine suggestion: For a red, Ochoa Tempranillo Granache Young Wine, or for a white, Mar de Frades Albarino*

# The Basque Market's Seafood Paella

When peeling shrimp, you may save the shells to add to your broth for an additional seafood flavor. You can also make your own fish broth using the shrimp shells and any fish carcasses you may have, thus leaving out the chicken broth entirely.

## Ingredients

- 6 *cups chicken or fish broth*
- 12 *strands saffron*
- 2 *tablespoons olive oil*
- ½ *onion, diced*
- 2-3 *garlic cloves, chopped*
- ½ *green pepper, diced*
- 1 *pound cod filet, cut into 1-inch pieces*
- 2 *cups medium rice*
- ½ *cup pimientos, diced*
- ½ *cup frozen peas and carrots*
- 1 *pound clams or cockles*
- ½ *pound mussels*
- ½ *pound scallops*
- ¾ *pound shrimp, peeled and deveined*

## Preparation

HEAT the broth and saffron to a low heat on back burner. You will be adding this in batches.

ADD the oil to a paella pan for 8 people and turn heat to medium-low. Sauté the onion until it is translucent, about 10 minutes. Add garlic and cook until aroma is noticeable. Add green peppers and cook about 5 minutes, making sure the vegetables do not brown. Add the cod and lightly sear on two sides. Remove cod and set aside. Add rice and stir well. Add about one-half to two-thirds of the broth, leaving the rest to simmer. Add pimientos and peas and carrots. Mix everything well so that the rice is at an even depth throughout the pan. Add clams, mussels, scallops, shrimp, and cod so that they are dispersed evenly throughout the pan. Do not stir rice from this point on. Add about one-half of the remaining broth and continue cooking until rice is done. You may need to continue adding more broth to make sure the rice finishes. Remove from heat and let rest for about 10 minutes before serving.

***Serves 8 – 10***

*Wine suggestion: Santiago Ruiz Albarino or Sumarroca Dry Muscat, from the Penedes region of Spain*

# Roasted Leg of Lamb

*with White Wine Sauce*

## Ingredients

- 1 *6- to 8-pound boneless leg of lamb*
- 1–2 *tablespoons coarse or kosher salt*
- 6 *cloves garlic, minced*
- 1 *tablespoon coarse black pepper*
- ¼ *cup olive oil*
- 4 *sprigs fresh rosemary, chopped (optional)*
- 2 *cups white wine, divided*
- 1 *14-ounce can beef broth*
- ½ *cup cold water*
- ¼ *cup cornstarch*

## Preparation

HEAT oven to 425 degrees. Remove netting from lamb and discard. Rinse lamb and pat dry. Open leg and remove connecting strip, if necessary. Butterfly the leg and remove pockets of fat on the inside part of the leg. Turn leg over and remove part of the thick layer of fat on the outside. Make a paste with the salt, garlic, pepper, and olive oil. Using a rubber glove or plastic baggie over your hand, rub the paste over the lamb, inside and out.

PLACE lamb flat onto a baking dish and put in 425-degree oven. After about 15 minutes, reduce heat to 350 degrees. After another 15 minutes, pour 1 cup of the white wine over the lamb. Continue roasting for another 15 minutes for medium rare or 30 minutes for medium. When the lamb has reached the desired temperature remove it from the oven and place it on a dish. Tent the lamb with foil while you make the sauce.

REDUCE the drippings from the lamb and add beef broth and the remaining wine. Simmer for about 10 minutes. Mix the cornstarch and water, and add to the sauce. Bring mixture back to a boil and let it thicken. Slice lamb and spoon sauce over top.

***Serves 12 – 16***

*Wine suggestions: Sumarroca Rosé, Ochoa Granache/Tempranillo, or Marques de Caceres Reserva*

# Arroz con Leche (Rice Pudding)

## Ingredients

- *½ gallon whole milk*
- *¾ cup Blue Rose rice*
- *2 small cinnamon sticks*
- *1 cup sugar*
- *ground cinnamon for garnish*

## Preparation

MIX milk, rice, and cinnamon sticks in heavy-bottomed pot, approximately 3 times the volume of the amount of milk used. Heat at medium heat until milk comes to a boil, about 15 minutes. Throughout this process, you must stir the mixture every few minutes to keep it from sticking. Once milk comes to a boil, reduce heat so that the milk remains at a low simmer.

AFTER 45 minutes from the start, add the sugar. Continue cooking until the milk starts to form large bubbles that remain for a second or two before bursting. This should take another 15-30 minutes. Remove from stove and ladle into a large bowl or separate servings. Sprinkle the top with ground cinnamon. Serve chilled or warm. Cover to keep a thick skin from forming.

***Serves 8***

THE
BASQUE MARKET
SPECIALIZING IN WINES • FOODS • GIFTS FROM THE IBERIAN PENINSULA

# Cottonwood Grille

913 W. River Street
Boise, ID 83702
208-333-9800
www.cottonwoodgrille.com

Lunch daily 11:00am to 4:00pm
Dinner daily 5:00pm to 10:00pm
Sunday Brunch 11:00am to 4:00pm

# Cottonwood Grille

***Peter Blatz, Owner/Chef***
***Hilary Blatz, Owner***

A meal at the Cottonwood Grille is a special experience, enlivening all the senses. As you walk into the restaurant, you are struck by the warm and comfortable luxury of your surroundings. The lounge offers you a choice of enjoying a pre-dinner libation in the comfort of the leather covered raised booths, at the wide wrap-around bar, or in an intimate corner sinking back into an overstuffed leather couch. But walking into the main dining room will take your breath away any time of the year. The spectacular massive stone fireplace set in the middle of floor-to-ceiling glass walls overlooking the cottonwood-lined Boise River sets the stage for an evening filled with fine food, fine wine, and immaculate yet discreet service. A comprehensive wine list specializing in the wines of California and Italy complement the wide variety of contemporary American cuisine, and have earned the restaurant Award of Excellence from the Wine Spectator since 2002.

This lovely restaurant was established in 1999 under the direction of Hilary and Peter Blatz, in partnership with the Hormaechea family of Boise. Chef Blatz has built the menu around his love for fresh ingredients and "made-from-scratch" cooking. In the restaurant business since the age of 15, he has worked with some of the finest chefs in New York and Connecticut. He pursued classical French cooking, working as saucier under Christian Bertrand at Bertrand's in Greenwich, CT. Later, he took on the saucier role for Robert Mazan of Le Cremailere and La Caravel in New York. He then worked as Chef de Cuisine for Pierre Nelie and Chez Pierre in Westport, CT. These committed chefs taught Peter the foundation and principles of cooking. He then built on that experience at the French Culinary Institute in New York.

After a successful career in New York, he moved to California and immersed himself in West Coast cuisine at the prestigious Dunes Restaurant at the Pebble Beach Resort. After several more years in California, including serving as the Executive Chef at The Bay Beach Café in Coronado, Peter returned to his French roots as General Manager of Denver's Le Central. During a visit to Boise, a twist of fate presented him with an opportunity to open his own restaurant in the city. This has given him a chance to put his extensive experience with classical French culinary techniques and West Coast knowledge of the advantage of using fresh ingredients to great use in the culinary philosophy of the Cottonwood Grille.

# Curried Lentil Soup

## Ingredients

- ¼ *cup olive oil*
- 2 *tablespoons fresh ginger, minced*
- 2 *tablespoons garlic, minced*
- 1 *cup onion, medium dice*
- 1 *cup carrot, medium dice*
- 1 *cup celery, medium dice*
- 1 *cup sweet potato, medium dice*
- 1 *tablespoon fresh curry powder*
- 1 *bunch cilantro, minced*
- 1 *cup yellow squash, medium dice*
- 1 *cup zucchini, medium dice*
- 1 *cup russet potato, medium dice*
- 1 *cup ripe tomato, medium dice*
- 2 *medium jalapenos, sliced (optional)*
- 3 *cups lentils, washed*
- 1½ *gallons water*
- *salt and pepper to taste*

## Preparation

IN A large, 1-gallon-plus heavy-bottomed saucepan, heat the olive oil until it ripples on the surface. Add ginger and sauté for 2 to 3 minutes. Add garlic and sauté until both ingredients start to caramelize. Add onion, carrot, celery, and sweet potatoes. Sauté until vegetables start to sweat. Next add curry and cilantro and continue to sauté. Finally add the rest of the ingredients and let the lentils cook until tender, or beyond, if you wish to give the soup a creamier consistency. Be sure to check the potatoes to make sure they are tender. Adjust seasonings and serve.

***Serves 6***

*Curried Lentil Soup*

# Seared Sea Scallops with Saffron Sauce

The amounts in this recipe are for serving one person. Just multiply the ingredients for the number of people you are serving.

## Ingredients

*5 U-10 untreated fresh scallops*
*flour*
*salt and pepper to taste*
*1 ounce olive oil*
*4 ounces fresh leaf spinach*
*1 teaspoon butter*
*½ shallot, chopped*
*4 ounces fresh angel hair pasta*
*3 ounces Saffron Sauce (recipe follows)*
*chopped chives for garnish*

## Preparation

HEAT oven to 300 degrees. Season the scallops with salt and pepper, and lightly dust them in the flour. Heat olive oil in a thick stainless steel sauté pan and add the scallops. Cook until golden and allow to rest. Do not wash pan; keep for the Saffron Sauce.

IN ANOTHER sauté pan, cook the shallots with the butter until the shallots are golden. Add spinach. It will cook very quickly and should be removed from the pan immediately. Place the cooked spinach on a plate in 5 small nests around the outer rim of the plate. Place the scallops on the spinach and keep warm in oven.

COOK the pasta in boiling water, strain, and add to the Saffron Sauce. Adjust seasonings and swirl in the center of the scallop plate. Garnish with chives.

***Serves 1***

*Wine suggestion: Duckhorn Sauvignon Blanc*

## For the Saffron Sauce

*1 ounce butter*
*1 tablespoon shallots, chopped*
*⅓ cup dry white wine*
*1 pinch saffron threads*
*⅓ cup fish fumet*
*½ cup heavy cream*
*salt and white pepper to taste*
*2 ounces chives, chopped*

IN THE pan used to sauté scallops, add the butter and shallots and sweat. Deglaze with white wine and add saffron and fumet. Reduce and add cream. Season with salt and white pepper and finish with chives.

# Nut Crusted Idaho Trout

*with Mango Salsa*

## Ingredients

- *1 large fresh Idaho trout filet*
- *¼ cup toasted peanuts*
- *¼ cup toasted filberts*
- *1 tablespoon curry powder*
- *1 tablespoon turmeric*
- *salt to taste*
- *¼ cup flour, divided*
- *1 egg, beaten*
- *olive oil*
- *Mango Salsa (recipe follows)*

## Preparation

IN A food processor, pulse the nuts and spices with 2 tablespoons of the flour until well mixed and the nuts are in small chunks. Set this mixture in a bowl. Season trout filet and dredge in the remaining flour. Dust off any excess and dip in the beaten egg. Remove, and dredge in the nut mixture. Sauté in olive oil until golden on both sides. If necessary, finish trout in 350-degree oven. Serve with Mango Salsa.

***Serves 1 trout per person***

*Wine suggestion: Elk Grove Pinot Gris*

## For the Mango Salsa

- *1 cup fresh mango, chopped*
- *2 ounces red onion, chopped*
- *2 ounces red bell pepper, chopped*
- *2 ounces green bell pepper, chopped*
- *½ fresh jalapeno, chopped*
- *1 tablespoon cilantro, chopped*
- *1 ounce extra virgin olive oil*
- *salt to taste*

COMBINE all ingredients and toss to coat with olive oil.

# Elk Wellington

*with Perigourdine Sauce and Mushroom Duxelle*

## Ingredients

- *1 elk tenderloin*
- *salt and pepper to taste*
- *8 ounces Mushroom Duxelle (recipe follows)*
- *1 pound liver pâté*
- *1 sheet puff pastry*
- *1 egg, beaten for egg wash*
- *Perigourdine Sauce (recipe follows)*

## Preparation

SEASON tenderloin with salt and freshly ground black pepper. In a hot pan, sear tenderloin on all sides. Set in cooler.

HEAT oven to 400 degrees. Roll out the puff pastry sheet and position cooled tenderloin at the bottom of the sheet, so that there is enough dough to wrap around the meat. Spread Mushroom Duxelle and liver pâté evenly over tenderloin. Brush the egg wash on the puff pastry around the meat and wrap the pastry around the tenderloin. Place on a baking pan lined with parchment paper and coat with the rest of the egg. Bake in 400-degree oven for 15 to 20 minutes. Allow to rest 10 minutes, slice, and serve with Perigourdine Sauce.

***Serves 8***

*Wine suggestion: Merry Edwards Russian River Valley Pinot Noir*

## For the Mushroom Duxelle

- *1 tablespoon garlic, chopped*
- *1 tablespoon butter*
- *1 tablespoon shallots, chopped*
- *½ cup shiitake mushrooms, sliced*
- *½ cup oyster mushrooms, sliced*
- *½ cup fresh morels*
- *1 splash brandy*
- *salt and pepper to taste*
- *1 ounce heavy cream*

IN A thick-bottomed non-reactive pot, sauté the garlic in the butter until golden. Add shallots, sweat, and then add mushrooms. Cook until the mushrooms release their liquid and start to dry. Deglaze with brandy, flame, add the cream, and reduce. Adjust seasoning with salt and pepper. Transfer to a food processor and purée until smooth. Set aside.

## For the Perigourdine Sauce

*1 tablespoon shallots, chopped*
*1 tablespoon butter*
*½ cup red wine*
*2 cups demi-glace*
*salt and pepper to taste*
*4 ounces foie gras, chopped*
*1 ounce black truffles, chopped*

IN A sauté pan, sweat the shallots in butter, deglaze with wine and reduce. Add the demi-glace, season with salt and pepper, and strain the mixture through a filter. Add the foie gras and truffles.

*Elk Wellington*

*Nut Crusted Idaho Trout*

# Chocolate Box

The result you want to achieve with this dessert is a square piece of cake inside chocolate walls that are slightly higher than the cake, with the top filled with whipped cream and fruit.

## Ingredients

*4 ounces butter, room temperature*
*1 cup sugar*
*2 large eggs*
*1 teaspoon vanilla*
*⅓ cup cake flour*
*1 teaspoon baking powder*
*1 pinch salt*
*½ cup milk*
*Caramel Sauce (recipe follows)*
*Chocolate Walls (recipe follows)*
*whipped cream*
*melted chocolate*
*strawberries*
*powdered sugar, for garnish*

## Preparation

HEAT oven to 350 degrees. Grease and lightly flour a square cake pan. Cream butter and sugar for 5 minutes. Add 1 egg at a time and the vanilla. Sift together the cake flour, baking flour, and salt 3 times. Alternate, in 3 batches, adding dry ingredients and milk to the butter mixture until completely incorporated. Do not over mix. Bake in 350-degree oven until toothpick can be removed clean, approximately 15 minutes. Let cake cool.

LAYER cake with whipped cream and Caramel Sauce and place in refrigerator to set. When set, cut cake into 3-inch squares. To assemble boxes, place a piece of 3-inch cake on your work surface. Position the Chocolate Walls around the cake, standing up, sticking it together with melted chocolate. When each box is assembled, fill in the tops with whipped cream and strawberries. Dust with powdered sugar.

***Yield: 6 3-inch by 3-inch boxes***

## For the Caramel Sauce

*1 cup sugar*
*¼ cup water*
*¾ cup heavy cream*

IN A thick-bottomed stainless steel pot, cook the sugar and water until it reaches medium amber in color. Add the cream slowly and whisk until smooth. Let cool.

## For the Chocolate Walls

*1 pound dark coating chocolate*

CHOP chocolate into chunks and melt in a double boiler to 88 degrees, being careful not to introduce any moisture. When chocolate reaches temperature, spread it evenly on parchment paper. Let cool and cut into rectangles with a warm paring knife.

# *Emilio's*

| The Grove Hotel | Lunch/Breakfast |
|---|---|
| 245 S. Capitol Blvd. | Monday - Friday 6:00am to 2:00pm |
| Boise, ID 83702 | Saturday - Sunday 7:00am to 2:00pm |
| 208-333-8000 | Dinner |
| www.grovehotelboise.com | Daily 5:00pm to 10:00pm |

# Emilio's

## *Rick Sordahl, Executive Chef*

The elegant Emilio's restaurant is a commanding part of the first floor of The Grove Hotel in downtown Boise and not to be considered like many "hotel restaurants". The European elegance of the entry warms the guests with cherry-paneled walls, neoclassical chandeliers, and brass accents. The adjoining lobby bar encourages lingering in overstuffed sofas, and chairs around the fireplace. With the open design of the restaurant, guests can enjoy the relaxing music of the pianist who plays every afternoon and evening in the bar.

Under the watchful eye of Executive Chef Rick Sordahl, Emilio's has expanded its culinary diversity, incorporating many international styles and fusing them with regional and local offerings, using only the freshest ingredients. Chef Sordahl has attained his high degree of experience by working in venues throughout the country, including restaurants in New Mexico, Arizona, Michigan, Florida, Nevada, and North Carolina. In Las Vegas, he was recognized by Zagat's with a *Top Ten Award* in 2000. At the prestigious Washington Duke Inn and Golf Club in Durham, North Carolina, he was awarded both the AAA *Four Diamond Award* and the Mobil Four Star Rating for three years in a row.

From the moment you are seated in the spacious and comfortable dining room, you will be pampered with the knowledgeable, attentive, yet discreet wait staff. The comfortable, plush chairs and banquettes complemented by the white linen service and the beautiful floral arrangements will set you at ease immediately. The extensive menu will tempt you with many mouth-watering items, from the fresh seafood flown in daily from Seattle to the excellent selection of well-aged steaks. You will also find an exceptional wine cellar of surprising depth. With over 450 wines by the bottle and an extensive "by the glass" program from which to choose, you and your guests will be able to find the perfect libations to compliment your culinary choices. This far-reaching wine collection has earned Emilio's the *Wine Spectator's Award of Excellence* for 2 years in a row.

Award of Excellence

# Sake Glazed Ginger Peaches & Huckleberry Cobbler

*with Pine Nut Streusel & Green Tea Ice Cream*

## Ingredients

- 2 *ounces fresh ginger, finely chopped*
- 6 *ounces sake rice wine*
- 6 *ounces sugar*
- 1 *vanilla bean split and scraped*
- ½ *star anise*
- 2½ *pounds IQF frozen peaches, sliced*
- 1½ *pounds huckleberries*
- *Pine Nut Streusel (recipe follows)*
- *Green Tea Ice Cream (recipe follows)*
- *peach slices for garnish*

## Preparation

PLACE ginger in saucepan with sake, sugar, vanilla bean, and star anise. Reduce to a syrup. Fold in peaches and cook until glazed, but not broken apart. Add huckleberries, and fold in. Refrigerate until cool. Remove star anise and vanilla bean.

WHEN ready to serve, heat oven to 350 degrees. Fill soufflé cups with peach-huckleberry cobbler mix to ½ inch from the top. Fill remainder with Pine Nut Streusel. Bake at 350 degrees for 10-15 minutes, until golden brown and hot in center. Cool for a couple of minutes. Add scoop of Green Tea Ice Cream on top, and garnish with a peach fan.

## For the Pine Nut Streusel

- 4 *ounces light brown sugar*
- 2 *ounces granulated sugar*
- 6 *ounces cake flour*
- 6 *ounces bread flour*
- 7 *ounces unsalted butter*
- 2 *ounces oatmeal*
- 2 *ounces pine nuts, coarse chopped*
- ½ *tablespoon ground cinnamon*

MIX together sugars and flours. Add butter, oatmeal, nuts, and cinnamon, cutting until just combined. Do not over mix or it will become one mass lump. Set aside.

## For the Green Tea Ice Cream

- 6 *cups heavy cream*
- 3 *cups 2% milk*
- ¾ *teaspoon salt*
- 18 *large eggs*
- 2¼ *cups sugar*
- 4½ *fluid ounces green tea Japanese matcha*

BRING cream, milk, and salt to boil in heavy saucepan. Remove from heat. Whisk eggs, sugar, and tea in mixing bowl. Slowly whisk milk mixture into egg mixture, stirring constantly. Cook over medium heat in heavy saucepan until 170 degrees, or thick enough to coat a spoon. Strain, cool overnight and freeze in ice cream machine. ***Yield: 3 quarts***

***Serves 14***

*Wine suggestions: Ste. Chapelle Ice Wine Riesling, Idaho or Three Rivers Winery Late Harvest Riesling Gewürztraminer, Biscuit Ridge Vineyard, Washington*

# Dungeness Crab Cakes

*with Carrot Fennel Slaw and Pink Grapefruit Aioli*

## Ingredients

- *2½ pounds Dungeness crab meat, drained*
- *1½ large eggs*
- *1½ teaspoons Dijon mustard*
- *1 tablespoon Old Bay Seasoning*
- *1¼ ounces lemon juice*
- *½ dash Tabasco sauce*
- *6 fluid ounces mayonnaise*
- *2 tablespoons fresh chives, minced*
- *1½ cups Japanese breadcrumbs*
- *salt & pepper to taste*
- *1 tablespoon cottonseed oil*
- *Carrot Fennel Slaw with Yuzu Dressing (recipes follows)*
- *Carrot Mint Sauce (recipe follows)*
- *Pink Grapefruit Aioli (recipe follows)*
- *Pink grapefruit sections for garnish*
- *micro cilantro for garnish*

## Preparation

PICK through crab for shells, but do not break up pieces. Mix egg, mustard, seasoning, lemon juice, Tabasco, mayonnaise, and chives together. Add crab and mix thoroughly. Add breadcrumbs, mix thoroughly, and season to taste. Separate mixture into 2- to 3-ounce patties.

HEAT sauté pan on medium heat, lightly coat with cottonseed oil. Sauté crab cakes until golden brown, about 2 – 3 minutes each side.

TO SERVE, arrange Carrot Fennel Slaw in a mound in center of plate, lean 2 crab cakes up against slaw and pool sauce around cakes. Arrange 3 grapefruit sections in front of crab cakes and drizzle Pink Grapefruit Aioli over top, garnishing with micro cilantro.

***Servings 8 to 10 as an appetizer***

*Wine suggestions: Hell's Canyon Bird Dog White, Idaho or Koenig Viognier, Idaho*

## For the Carrot Fennel Slaw

- *8 ounces carrot, fine julienne*
- *2 ounces fennel bulb, fine julienne*
- *4 ounces jicama, fine julienne*
- *2 ounces red onion, fine julienne*
- *2 tablespoons fresh mint, julienne*
- *½ tablespoon shallots, chopped*
- *½ teaspoon honey*
- *4 ounces apricot nectar*
- *1 tablespoon Dijon mustard*
- *2 fluid ounces balsamic white vinegar*
- *¼ ounce lemon juice*
- *1½ teaspoon yuzu powder*
- *½ tablespoon fresh chives, chopped*
- *3½ ounces canola or olive oil*
- *salt and pepper to taste*

THOROUGHLY mix the carrot, fennel, jicama, onion, and mint in a bowl. Combine the rest of the ingredients except the oil in a blender or food processor. Slowly drizzle in the oil until the mixture is completely emulsified. Add salt and pepper to taste. Add about 2 ounces of the dressing to slaw and stir to combine. Keep cool until ready to serve.

### For the Carrot Mint Sauce

*2 cups carrot juice*
*½ cup unsweetened 100% orange juice*
*4 tablespoons lemongrass, finely chopped*
*1 sprig fresh mint*
*2 ounces whole butter*

IN A pan, combine the juices, lemongrass, and mint. Reduce by half and finish with the butter.

### For the Pink Grapefruit Aioli

*5 ounces egg yolks*
*4 roasted garlic cloves*
*10 ounces extra virgin olive oil*
*1/10 7-ounce can chipotle whole pepper, chopped*
*dash Tabasco sauce*
*dash Worcestershire sauce*
*1 fluid ounce ruby red pink grapefruit juice*
*1 teaspoon pink grapefruit zest, chopped*
*salt and pepper to taste*

PUT egg yolks and garlic in blender and blend until light in color. Slowly add the oil and emulsify. Add chipotle and blend until puréed. Add remainder of ingredients and season with salt and pepper.

*Dungeness Crab Cakes*

# Mole Rubbed Wild Salmon

*with Black Bean Polenta, Cilantro Lime Spaghetti Squash, and Avocado Crème Fraîche*

## Ingredients

- *8 6-ounce Northwest wild salmon fillets*
- *2 tablespoons Spanish onion, diced*
- *1 ounce New Mexican dried chili*
- *1 cup water*
- *⅛ lime, juiced*
- *salt and pepper to taste*
- *Green Mole (recipe follows)*
- *Black Bean Polenta Cakes (recipe follows)*
- *Cilantro Lime Spaghetti Squash (recipe follows)*
- *Avocado Crème Fraîche (recipe follows)*
- *yucca root, julienned, for garnish*
- *parsley sprigs, for garnish*

## Preparation

SAUTÉ the onion until translucent, add chili and water, and reduce until most of the water has evaporated. Place the mixture in a blender and purée. Add limejuice and season to taste. Strain the mixture and reserve in a squirt bottle for final garnish.

RUB salmon fillets with Green Mole. Heat a non-stick sauté pan on medium heat and pan sear the fillets for 3 – 4 minutes, until caramelized on each side, and still moist in center.

TO SERVE, arrange to Black Bean Polenta Cakes in center of each plate. Add Cilantro Lime Spaghetti Squash on top of cakes. Next stack a salmon fillet on top. Stripe each plate with Avocado Crème Fraîche. Dot each plate with some of the reserved chili mixture. If available, garnish with julienned yucca root and parsley.

***Serves 6***

*Wine suggestions: Elk Grove Pinot Gris, Oregon or Koenig Syrah, Idaho*

## For the Green Mole

- *5 ounces sesame seeds*
- *1½ ounces dried pumpkin seeds*
- *3 whole cloves*
- *3 black peppercorns*
- *3 allspice berries*
- *2½ cups warm chicken stock, divided*
- *3 tablespoons vegetable oil*
- *2 garlic cloves*
- *6 ounces tomatillo, rough chopped*
- *2 roasted poblano chilies, peeled & seeded*
- *7 serrano chilies*
- *8 romaine lettuce leaves*
- *5 Swiss chard leaves*
- *1½ cups fresh cilantro, chopped*
- *½ cup Italian parsley, chopped*
- *salt and pepper to taste*

TOAST sesame seeds until golden brown. Don't burn. Let cool. Roast pumpkin seeds until they swell and pop around in pan. Let cool. Grind sesame seeds in spice mill with cloves, peppercorns, and allspice until powdered. Add pumpkin seeds and blend until finely chopped. Transfer to a mixing bowl and whisk in 1 cup of warm chicken stock, mixing until a thick paste is formed. Heat oil in heavy casserole, add seed paste, and cook over medium heat, stirring constantly until dry, shiny, rich golden brown color is achieved. Do not let mixture burn or stick to pot. Let cool.

IN FOOD processor, add garlic, tomatillo, chilies, and 1 cup warm chicken stock. Blend until smooth. Add romaine, chard, cilantro, and parsley, little by little, until all are incorporated and blended smooth. Add lettuce mixture to seed paste, return to heat, and let cook until reduced and thickened, about 10 to 20 minutes. Add extra warm chicken stock if needed. Season to taste.

## For the Black Bean Polenta

*16 ounces 2% milk*
*16 ounces water*
*10 ounces polenta*
*½ cup black beans, cooked*
*¼ tablespoon ground coriander*
*¼ teaspoon paprika*
*¼ teaspoon fresh oregano, chopped*
*1 fluid ounce Manchego cheese, shredded*
*salt and pepper to taste*

BRING water and milk to a boil. Gradually whisk in polenta until fully incorporated. Bring to a simmer over medium heat. Reduce heat to low and cook for about 45 minutes, stirring frequently. Remove from heat and whisk in remaining ingredients. Pour into a hotel pan and cool immediately. Cut cooled polenta into 2- to 3-inch circles. Pan sear the cakes until golden brown on each side. Keep warm in oven for service.

## For the Cilantro Lime Spaghetti Squash

*24 ounces spaghetti squash, cooked and shredded*
*2 limes, juiced*
*6 teaspoons garlic, chopped*
*6 tablespoons butter, room temperature*
*½ cup fresh cilantro, chopped*
*salt and pepper to taste*

HEAT pan, add whole butter and sauté garlic. Add squash and cook until hot. Add rest of ingredients and season to taste.

## For the Avocado Crème Fraîche

*1 cup avocado pulp*
*2 cups crème fraîche*
*½ teaspoon ground cumin*
*½ teaspoon paprika*
*1 teaspoon lime juice*
*salt and pepper to taste*

COMBINE all ingredients except crème fraîche and mix until smooth. Ass crème fraîche, mix thoroughly, and season to taste. Hold in a squirt bottle for service.

# Roasted Chicken Breast

*with Riesling Jam, Madeira Jus, and Parsnip Mash*

## Ingredients

4 *free range chicken breasts, split in half, frenched, with wing bone attached*
*salt and pepper to taste*
*vegetable oil*
*wilted baby spinach, sautéed with garlic, salt, & white pepper*
*Riesling Jam (recipe follows)*
*Madeira Jus (recipe follows)*
*Parsnip Mash (recipe follows)*

## Preparation

HEAT oven to 350 degrees. Season chicken breasts with salt and pepper. Heat sauté pan on medium, with a little vegetable oil. Add chicken breasts, skin side down, and sauté for 4–6 minutes until golden brown. Flip breast over, sauté for a minute, and finish in 350-degree oven for 6-10 minutes until done. Keep moist, 155-165 degrees temperature in center of meat.

TO SERVE, pipe Parsnip Mash on center of plate. Serve with wilted baby spinach sautéed with garlic, salt and pepper. Prop chicken breast against the Parsnip Mash and spinach, with the wing bone at top. Nap front of chicken with Madeira Jus and put a dollop of Riesling Jam across chicken.

***Serves 8***

*Wine suggestions: Chateau Ste. Michelle "Dr. Loosen Eroica", Washington or Hell's Canyon Reserve Merlot, Idaho*

## For the Riesling Jam

2 *cups Riesling wine*
6 *cups Thompson grapes, halved*
¼ *cup honey*
2 *tablespoons white sugar*
2 *tablespoons brown sugar*
1 *cinnamon stick*
¼ *cup shallots, sliced*
*zest of 2 navel oranges*

COMBINE all ingredients and reduce to a syrup consistency. Remove cinnamon stick.

## For the Madeira Jus

2 *ounces chicken bones, chopped*
1 *teaspoon vegetable oil*
1 *shallot, thinly sliced*
¾ *teaspoon garlic, chopped*
7 *ounces Madeira wine*
16 *ounces veal demi-glace*
¼ *teaspoon fresh thyme*
¼ *bay leaf*
*whole butter, to finish*
*salt and pepper to taste*

OVER medium-high heat, brown the chicken bones in the oil. Add shallot and garlic and cook until translucent. Add the wine and reduce liquid by 80%. Add demi-glace and the aromatics and simmer until sauce coats a spoon. Strain through a chinois and simmer. When ready to serve, finish the sauce with salt, pepper, and whole butter.

## For the Parsnip Mash

- *12 ounces Idaho 60-ct potatoes, peeled*
- *20 ounces parsnips, peeled*
- *¼ tablespoon white whole peppercorn, ground*
- *1 tablespoon kosher salt*
- *6 ounces unsalted butter, softened*
- *2 ounces sour cream*
- *2 ounces heavy cream*
- *1 tablespoon green onion, chopped*

PUT potatoes and parsnips in separate pots, and cover with cool water. Bring both pots to a boil over high heat and simmer contents until cooked through. Strain potatoes and parsnips, and allow potatoes to dry. Grind parsnips in meat grinder with fine die. In a large bowl, combine salt, pepper, butter, and sour cream. Add potatoes, mash thoroughly, and fold in parsnip. Add heavy cream gradually to desired consistency. Adjust seasonings. Wrap and store in hotbox. Work quickly so that potatoes stay hot.

*Roasted Chicken Breast*

*Lee Morehouse ca. 1890's*

# The Gamekeeper Restaurant

1109 Main Street
Boise, ID 83702
Located in the Owyhee Plaza Hotel
208-343-4611
www.owyheeplaza.com

Dinner
Monday - Saturday 5:00pm to 10:00pm
Reservations recommended

# The Gamekeeper Restaurant

### *Mark Owsley, Head Chef*
### *John May, General Manager*
### *Dean Hanson, Maitre d'*

The Gamekeeper's history reaches back to the early 1900s, and to an era when, in the words of General Manager John May, "fine dining once meant that your dinner experience was the highlight and entertainment of your evening, and not just a quick meal on the way to wherever you were going." To recapture that experience, the Gamekeeper maintains a culinary tradition of elegance, continental cuisine, tableside preparation and entrées that are exceptional. Sadly, these traditions were nearly lost in the late 80s. With the acquisition of the hotel and restaurant by the May family and their partners, the restaurant returned to its roots.

Fortunately for the Mays, they inherited a seasoned staff that felt a similar passion about the restaurant, including highly regarded Head Chef Mark Owsley, and Maitre d' Hanson. Much of what makes the Gamekeeper experience so unique – and so memorable – is the tableside preparation that marks so many of its dishes, from its signature Caesar Salad to house favorites such as Steak Diane, to classic flambé desserts such as Bananas Foster and Cherries Jubilee. Be prepared for pyrotechnic displays of three to four foot high flames. In keeping with its name, the Gamekeeper menu includes entrées such as elk and buffalo – the latter of which has become increasingly popular since its introduction.

With dishes that have withstood the test of time and defined the Gamekeeper's fine dining reputation, the Mays have kept the core of the restaurant's menu consistent, with Chef Owsley and Maitre d' Hanson coming together to add seasonal favorites.

An enormously popular addition to the Gamekeeper's regular fare are its monthly wine dinners, which perfectly match a gourmet seven-course menu with wines from some of the finest cellars in the world. These events, which take place the second Sunday of each month, sell out quickly. And in the best Gamekeeper tradition, says John May, "come for the evening, sit back, relax and enjoy...by the way, we can even get you a nice room if you would like to stay the night."

# Maple Roasted Salmon

*with Maple Cream Sauce*

## Ingredients

- *6 7-ounce salmon filets, ½- to ¾-inch thick*
- *2 ounces fresh ginger, finely diced*
- *1 tablespoon honey*
- *2 tablespoons olive oil*
- *2 tablespoons crushed peppercorn blend*
- *¼ cup butter*
- *¼ cup maple syrup*
- *Maple Cream Sauce (recipe follows)*
- *finely chopped parsley or scallion curls for garnish*

## Preparation

HEAT oven to 450 degrees. Place ginger, honey, and olive oil in blender and blend until a paste consistency is achieved. Rub ginger paste on both sides of salmon filets and lightly season with crushed peppercorns.

MELT butter in frying pan and add salmon filets, searing each side for approximately 1 minute. Place filets on a lightly buttered sheet pan and bake in 450-degree oven for 8 minutes. Remove from oven and brush filets with maple syrup, then bake 2 more minutes. Salmon filets should be moist inside.

TO SERVE, ladle Maple Cream Sauce onto plates. Place salmon filets on top of sauce and drizzle a little more sauce on top. Garnish with fine chopped parsley or scallion curls.

***Serves 6***

*Wine suggestion: Penfolds Bin 128 Coonawarra Shiraz*

## For the Maple Cream Sauce

- *1 cup heavy cream*
- *½ cup maple syrup*
- *2 tablespoons sour cream*

PLACE heavy cream and maple syrup in saucepan and simmer until reduced by half, or until slightly thickened. Remove from heat and whisk in sour cream until mixture is smooth. If sauce is too thick, whisk in a small amount of warm water. Keep warm until ready to serve.

# Dijon Crusted Rack of Lamb

## Ingredients

- 1 14-ounce domestic rack of lamb, Frenched
- ¼ cup flour, seasoned with salt and white pepper
- 1 ounce Dijon mustard
- ¼ cup panko breadcrumbs
- 1 ounce drawn (clarified) butter
- 2 ounces apple mint jelly

## Preparation

HEAT oven to 425 degrees. Dust lamb rack with seasoned flour. Coat rack with Dijon mustard and then cover with panko. Lightly drizzle drawn butter over the rack. Place in a pan and bake in the 425-degree oven for about 25 minutes. Pull rack out of oven and let rest for 5 minutes. Rack should be a good medium rare. Slice between bones and present on a plate with the apple mint jelly.

***Serves 1***

*Wine suggestion: Patz & Hall Hyde Vineyard Pinot Noir*

# Peaches and Cream Duck

## Ingredients

*4 5-ounce duck breasts*
*4 ounces vegetable oil*
*1 ounce honey*
*3 ounces peach schnapps, divided*
*1 ounce water*
*4 ounces heavy cream*
*1 tablespoon sour cream*
*1 ripe peach*
*fresh fine chopped parsley for garnish*

## Preparation

HEAT oven to 400 degrees. Heat the vegetable oil in an 8-inch frying pan. Oil should reach 325 degrees, but do not let it get too hot. Place duck breasts, fat side down, in the pan. Cook for about 3 – 5 minutes, until the duck gets crispy on the bottom. Turn duck over and cook for 2 more minutes. Discard oil. Top ducks with honey, 1 ounce of the peach schnapps, and 1 ounce of water. Place in 400-degree oven for 6 minutes to finish.

COMBINE the rest of the peach schnapps with the heavy cream in a saucepan. Bring to a simmer and reduce by about half, or until the mixture slightly thickens. Whisk in the sour cream until smooth and set aside.

REMOVE ducks from oven and let rest for a couple of minutes. Duck breasts should be medium rare. Slice each duck into about 5 slices. Quarter the peach and slice each quarter into 4 slices. Place a peach slice in between each duck slice. Divide sauce onto 4 plates and present the duck/peach combination on top of the sauce. Garnish with fresh parsley.

***Serves 4***

*Wine suggestion: Cakebread Chardonnay*

# Rocky Mountain Elk

## Ingredients

- 8 *3-ounce elk tenderloin medallions*
  *coarse black pepper and salt*
- 6 *ounces brown sauce*
- 4 *ounces crème de cassis*
- 1 *cup fresh blackberries*
- 2 *ounces butter*
  *fresh rosemary sprigs for garnish*

## Preparation

IN A saucepan, combine brown sauce and crème de cassis and reduce by one third. Sauce should slightly thicken. Remove from heat and add blackberries. Presentation is better if the blackberries are left whole in the sauce. Keep warm.

POUND out elk medallions to about ¼-inch thickness. Lightly season with pepper and a little salt. Heat a frying pan and melt butter. Sauté elk medallions for about 1 – 2 minutes per side, and remove from pan. It is important to not overcook them. Medium rare is best.

PLACE a little of the sauce on 4 individual plates. Place 2 medallions on each plate, top with a little more sauce and garnish with fresh rosemary sprigs.

***Serves 4***

*Wine suggestion: Jade Mountain Paras Syrah*

204 N Capitol Blvd.
Boise, ID 83702
208-336-0889

Monday: 7:00am to 3:00pm
Tuesday - Thursday: 7:00am to 10:00pm
Friday – Saturday: 7:00am to 1:00am
Sunday: 7:00am to 3:00pm

# Le Café de Paris

## *Mathieu Choux, Owner/Chef*

Enjoy a little bit of Paris in downtown Boise, at Le Café de Paris. This charming bistro is true French, thanks to the efforts of its owner and chef, Mathieu Choux. Originally from Burgundy, France, Mathieu's goal was to have a little French bistro and bakery. According to Mathieu, a bistro in France "is a place where you can have lunch or a drink in a nice but casual atmosphere". With that goal in mind, Mathieu opened Le Café de Paris in April 2002, serving breakfast and lunch. His culinary philosophy is based on recreating the flavors of France, making everything from scratch, using fresh, seasonal, and local ingredients.

With good food, an experienced wait staff, and a large wine list, the success of the bistro allowed Mathieu to expand the dining room and build a deck for outdoor seating in order to accommodate the growing ranks of culinary fans. Sitting on the deck in late spring or summer is a joyous experience as you take in the sights and sounds of downtown Boise, and gaze at the beautiful landscaping around the State Capitol building just north of the restaurant. Along with the expansion, Mathieu built a full kitchen in order to be open for dinner. October 2003 was the opening of the dinner menu that features traditional French bistro dishes such as Burgundy Style Beef Stew and Rack of Lamb. The wine list includes a large selection of wines and champagnes by the glass, including many prime choices from France as well as the rest of the world.

If you are looking for a place to hold a private dinner, Le Café de Paris has the perfect place. In the basement of the restaurant a banquet room has been designed. It is called Le Caveau (meaning cellar in French) because of its stone walls and cellar ambiance.

When you enter the bistro, you will be impressed with the mouth-watering display of fresh pastries that are made on the premises, along with fresh-baked breads. It will remind you to save room for one of these delights. Or, stop by after an evening out for a special dessert treat.

Mathieu attributes the success of his restaurant to his hard work and that of his dedicated front staff, manager Remi Courcenet, and his sous chef Alicia Whiteford.

# Thyme-Crusted Chilean Sea Bass

*with Tomato Concassé and Rice Pilaf*

## Ingredients

- *4 6-ounce portions fresh Chilean sea bass*
- *4 slices Thyme Butter (recipe follows)*
- *8 ounces dry white wine*
- *salt and pepper*
- *Tomato Concassé (recipe follows)*
- *Rice Pilaf (recipe follows)*

## Preparation

HEAT oven to 350 degrees. Place a slice of Thyme Butter on each piece of sea bass. Put the sea bass in an ovenproof dish that is just large enough to hold the bass. Add wine, salt and pepper, and poach in the oven for 10 minutes.

TO SERVE, remove the bass from the poaching liquid. Place a portion of Rice Pilaf on each plate. Place the sea bass resting slightly on the pilaf, and place the Tomato Concassé next to the bass.

***Serves 4***

## For the Thyme Butter

- *2 ounces fresh thyme*
- *8 ounces bread crumbs, really fine*
- *8 ounces butter, room temperature*
- *salt and pepper*

CLEAN and strip the thyme. Mix the butter with the breadcrumbs and the thyme. Add salt and pepper to taste. Form a little square and keep cool in the refrigerator.

## For the Tomato Concassé

- *4 tomatoes, chopped*
- *1 teaspoon herbes de Provence*
- *1 ounce fresh basil*
- *2 sprigs fresh thyme*
- *1 bay leaf*

IN A medium pot over medium heat, place all the ingredients and cook down. Season to taste.

## For the Rice Pilaf

- *4 ounces onions, diced*
- *3 ounces butter*
- *3 cups jasmine rice*
- *4½ cups chicken stock*
- *bouquet garni (parsley, thyme, and 3 bay leaves wrapped in a leaf of leek)*

HEAT oven to 350 degrees. Sauté the onions with the butter and then add the rice. Sauté for 5 more minutes. Add the chicken stock, bring to a boil, and put the pot in oven for 17 minutes with the bouquet garni and salt and pepper.

# Lamb Rack

*with Cognac and Demi-Glace Sauce and Garlic Mashed Potatoes*

## Ingredients

- *2 8-ounce lamb racks*
- *2 tablespoons herbes de Provence*
- *2 tablespoons fleur de sel*
- *clarified butter or vegetable oil*
- *Cognac and Demi-Glace Sauce (recipe follows)*
- *Garlic Mashed Potatoes (recipe follows)*

## Preparation

HEAT oven to 350 degrees. Rub the herbes de Provence on the lamb racks, followed by the fleur de sel. Preheat a sauté pan with clarified butter or vegetable oil. Sear the lamb racks and place in the 350-degree oven for 10 minutes for rare and 25 minutes for well done.

TO SERVE, spoon the sauce onto a plate and place the lamb rack on top. Add a scoop of the potatoes to the side, along with some steamed asparagus.

***Serves 2***

## For the Cognac and Demi-Glace Sauce

- *3 tablespoons shallots, minced*
- *butter*
- *2 ounces Cognac*
- *6 ounces beef demi-glace*
- *1 tablespoon beurre manié (mix together equal parts room temp butter and flour)*

SAUTÉ the shallots with some butter. Drain the butter and deglaze the pan with cognac. Adding the cognac to the warm pan will produce a flame, and catch the little particles at the bottom of the pan to add flavor to the sauce. Add the beef demi-glace and bring to a boil. Add beurre manié and stir. At this point, the more you boil the mixture, the more it will reduce and the thicker your sauce will be. Season to taste and keep warm.

## For the Garlic Mashed Potatoes

- *2 pounds Idaho potatoes, peeled and diced*
- *4 garlic cloves, diced really thin*
- *butter*
- *half and half cream*
- *salt and pepper to taste*

PUT the potatoes in a pot with water and salt. Bring to a boil and boil for 10 minutes, or until done. Drain potatoes and add diced garlic and butter. Mash potatoes using a potato masher. Add a little bit of half and half to desired consistency and season with salt and pepper.

# Burgundy Style Beef Stew

## Ingredients

- 2 *pounds beef stew meat*
- *vegetable oil*
- 4 *carrots, thinly sliced lengthwise*
- 1 *cup small button mushrooms, quartered*
- ½ *pound bacon, cut in small slices*
- ¼ *cup all-purpose flour*
- 1 *bottle Cabernet Sauvignon*
- 4 *cups beef stock*
- 4 *little branches thyme*
- 4 *bay leaves*
- *salt and pepper to taste*
- 2 *dozen pearl onions*

## Preparation

HEAT oven to 350 degrees. Sauté the bacon pieces in a skillet until crisp. Remove and drain bacon pieces. Preheat a pot with a little bit of vegetable oil. When warm, add the beef stew meat and sauté until each piece is golden brown on the outside.

ONCE the beef is sautéed, remove the pot from the burner and remove the liquid (if any) from the pot. Add the flour and mix to coat every piece of meat. Put the pot in the 350-degree oven for 5-8 minutes. Remove it from oven and stir the contents. Put it back in the oven for another 5-8 minutes. The flour will cook on the meat and will help to thicken the sauce.

PUT the pot back on the burner; add the carrots and the wine and stir to combine. If you need more liquid to cover the meat add the beef stock. Bring the mixture to a boil and add thyme, bay leaves, salt, pepper, pearl onions, and bacon.

COVER the pot and return to the 350-degree oven and cook until tender, about 1 hour and 20 to 40 minutes. Serve with fresh pasta.

***Serves 6 to 8***

*Wine suggestion: Any red wine from the Cote De Beaune area in Burgundy, France.*

# Filet Mignon

*in Crust with Parsley Green Beans and a Red Wine Reduction Sauce*

## Ingredients

*4 6- to 8-ounce filet mignon or 1 Chateaubriand*
*clarified butter*
*salt and pepper to taste*
*2 tablespoons shallots, diced*
*2 cups red wine*
*2 cups demi-glace*
*2 tablespoons beurre manié (equal parts room temperature butter & flour, mixed together*
*2 sheets puff pastry*
*1 egg*
*Parsley Green Beans (recipe follows)*

## Preparation

HEAT oven to 350 degrees. In a skillet, heat some clarified butter. Season the filets with salt and pepper, and pound them. Sear the filets on each side in the skillet, and remove them. Add the shallots to the skillet along with the red wine, and reduce the wine to two-thirds of its volume. Add the demi-glace. Let it simmer and then add the beurre manié, stirring to thoroughly combine. Bring back to a boil while stirring, and then remove from heat. Keep warm.

WRAP each filet mignon in puff pastry. Crack the egg in a small bowl and, with a brush or towel, paint the outside of the puff pastry. Put them on a sheet pan and place in the 350-degree oven until done: 5 minutes for medium rare, and 20 minutes for well done.

TO SERVE, ladle a portion of the red wine reduction on each plate. Place the filet mignon in the puff pastry on top of the sauce and surround with Parsley Green Beans.

***Serves 4***

*Wine suggestion: A good red Burgundy*

## For the Parsley Green Beans

*1 pound green beans*
*2 cloves garlic*
*6 sprigs parsley, chopped*
*butter*
*salt and pepper to taste*

CLEAN and remove both ends of each green bean. Put them in a pot with cold water. Blanch the vegetables by bringing the pot to a boil and boiling them for 4 minutes. Drain the beans and immediately run cold water over them, preferably with some ice. The process will cool them down fast and let them keep their bright green color. Warm up some butter in a sauté pan. Dry the green beans in a towel and add them to the sauté pan with the garlic. Sauté for 5 to 7 minutes, or until done. Season with salt and pepper and toss with the parsley.

# The Milky Way

In the Empire Building
205 North 10th Street #110
Boise, ID 83702
208-343-4334
www.milkywayboise.com

Lunch:
Monday – Friday 11:00am to 3:00pm
Dinner:
Monday – Thursday 5:00pm to 10:00pm
Friday – Saturday 5:00 to 12:00am

# The Milky Way

## *Mitchell and Andrea Maricich, Chef/Owners*

The chic atmosphere and delightful cuisine of The Milky Way is the result of a family collaboration. Chefs "Milky" Mitchell and Andrea opened the doors of their restaurant in July 2001, featuring a menu that appeals to the most sophisticated palate, as well as the casual diner. Designer Gary Maricich, Mitchell's brother, was brought in to handle the aesthetic features of the restaurant. Gary used local craftsmen and suppliers whose combined talents created such features as the Baltic birch cabinets and bar display, hand gold-leafed columns, and white granite tabletops. A spectacular contemporary chandelier hangs from the two-story ceiling through the opening created by the mezzanine level of the restaurant and lights the romantic two-person booth set near the front door. The booth has an upholstered back that circles up and around the two diners, creating a cozy cocoon effect.

At lunch and dinner, when the weather is pleasant, the glass walls of the restaurant that face 10th Street can be opened to let in the fresh air, and there is also patio dining available when the weather co-operates. On the mezzanine level, diners are seated at comfortable banquettes upholstered in a cheery red fabric that counterpoints the silver metallic chairs. And, because of the high glass windows that come all the way up to the mezzanine, diners can enjoy the city lights of this vibrant downtown area. Also on the mezzanine is a custom designed wine display room, featuring a large selection of over 150 international and domestic wines. The Milky Way features a fine selection of German beers, as well as local micro-brews and draft options, and has a full bar, offering a large number of martinis. It has become known for its "Ten Minute Martini™", the quintessential interpretation of this classic.

Mitchell, a graduate of the Culinary Institute of American in Hyde Park, New York, has over 20 years of experience in the restaurant industry. Andrea, a graduate of the New England Culinary Institute in Vermont, has over 19 years restaurant experience, and owned her own company, the Gourmet Brown Bag that provided gourmet lunch delivery service in and around Sausalito, California, as well as catering lunches for small businesses and large corporations. Their combined culinary experience includes work in some of California's fine dining venues, such as Postrio, Roti, Boulevard, and Fog City Diner.

# Jalapeno Shrimp Bites

*with Tomato Apricot Chutney*

This recipe is very simple. It can be prepared the day before and grilled right before serving. The recipe for the jalapenos themselves is only for one, multiply as necessary. Don't be shy. We promise, they will go surprisingly fast!

## Ingredients – for each jalapeno

- 1 *large fresh jalapeno pepper*
- 1 *piece jack cheese, cut to approximately 1 inch by ½ inch by ¼ inch*
- ½ *lengthwise-cut shrimp, peeled, deveined*
- ½ *slice smoky bacon*
- *Tomato Apricot Chutney (recipe follows)*

## Preparation

HEAT oven to 350 degrees. When preparing the jalapenos it is advisable to use gloves. Cut the top and stem off the jalapeno. Slice it lengthwise on one side, just to open the pepper, not to cut it in half. Carefully open pepper and scrape or cut out the seeds. Place jalapenos on a sheet tray and roast in 350-degree oven for 15 to 20 minutes. Let cool before stuffing.

PLACE the piece of cheese beside the shrimp half and enclose it in the jalapeno. Wrap pepper in the bacon and skewer. If the pepper should break when you put the shrimp in, the bacon wrap will hold it together. Place stuffed peppers on a lined baking sheet and place in 350-degree oven for 15 to 20 minutes, or until the bacon is crispy and the jalapeno is a bit tender. You can eat them now with the Tomato Apricot Chutney, or finish them on the grill later in the day, or even 2 or 3 days later.

## For the Tomato Apricot Chutney

- ½ *cup onion, minced*
- 5 *garlic cloves, minced*
- 1 *ounce olive oil*
- 2 *pounds fresh plum tomatoes, large dice*
- ¼ *pound dried apricots, medium dice*
- ¼ *cup cider vinegar*
- ¾ *cup sugar*
- ¼ *tablespoon yellow mustard seeds*
- ¼ *tablespoon black mustard seeds*
- 1 *bay leaf*
- ¼ *teaspoon white pepper*
- ½ *teaspoon salt*

SAUTÉ onion and garlic in the olive oil until onion is translucent. Add tomatoes and apricots and simmer for 5 minutes. Add rest of ingredients and simmer on low heat until the chutney is thickened. This can be made in advance and served at room temperature or reheated in a saucepan with a little water.

***Yield: 2 cups***

# Milky Way Clam Chowder

## Ingredients

- 1½ *pounds bacon, cut in small strips*
- ½ *bunch celery, small dice*
- 4 *cups onions, small dice*
- 1 *bunch scallions, bias cut*
- 1½ *cups all-purpose flour*
- 2 *51-ounce cans clam juice*
- 2 *cups white wine*
- 4 *cups red potatoes, medium dice*
- 2 *tablespoons fresh thyme, chopped fine*
- 2 *teaspoons cayenne pepper*
- 1 *bay leaf*
- 1 *51-ounce can chopped clams*
- 4 *shakes Tabasco sauce*
- 2 *quarts heavy cream*
- *salt and pepper to taste*

## Preparation

IN A large stockpot, cook bacon until golden brown. Add celery, onions, and scallions and sweat until translucent, about 5 minutes. Add flour and cook for 4 minutes, stirring constantly. Add clam juice and white wine and stir until there are no more chunks of flour left. Add rest of ingredients to stockpot; bring to a boil and then turn down to a simmer. Continue simmering until the potatoes are cooked. Season with salt and pepper and you are good to go.

***Yield: 2½ gallons***

# Lamb Stir Fry

## Ingredients

- 1 *large head radicchio*
- 1 *tablespoon sesame oil*
- 1 *pound ground lamb*
- 1 *tablespoon garlic, finely chopped*
- 1 *tablespoon fresh ginger, grated*
- 1 *tablespoon fresh mint, chopped*
- 1 *tablespoon fresh cilantro, chopped*
- 1½ *tablespoons soy sauce*
- 2 *tablespoons water*
- 1 *pinch chili flakes*

## Preparation

CORE radicchio head and make cups out of the leaves. Heat a sauté pan until almost to the smoking point. Add sesame oil and then the ground lamb, breaking it up into little pieces. Be careful not to splash hot oil on yourself. When meat is brown, drain excess fat from pan and add garlic, ginger, mint, and cilantro. Sauté for about 30 seconds. Add rest of ingredients and cook until almost dry.

TO SERVE, place lamb mixture in a large bowl with a serving spoon. Place radicchio leaves on a platter. Guests can scoop the lamb stir-fry into the radicchio cups and eat like a lettuce wrap.

***Serves 8 - 10***

*Wine suggestion: a full-bodied Pinot or Syrah*

# Beef Cheeks

These cheeks are a labor of love and take two days to create. Please read and prep ahead. The amount of meat looks like a lot to serve 10 to 12 people, but you will find that you will get about 10 pounds of trimmings that will be used in the stock, leaving only 10 pounds of beef cheeks that will also shrink as it is cooked. Enjoy this dish. Everyone in Boise loves them.

## Ingredients

*20 pounds beef cheeks*
*1 cup cooking oil*
*1 tablespoon kosher salt*
*½ tablespoon black pepper*
*½ pound red beets*
*½ bunch celery, chopped*
*6 pounds onions, chopped*
*6 ounces garlic, smashed*
*1 bunch fresh thyme*
*1 bunch fresh parsley*
*½ gallon red wine*
*1½ gallons beef stock*
*Vegetable Mix (recipe follows)*

## Preparation

TRIM beef cheeks by cutting the excess fat off along with the loose stuff. Turn the cheek so the back part is facing you and the flat part is on the bottom. It should look like you are looking down a tongue. Trim off the tip of the cheek. It looks like a fingernail or crescent moon. Save all the trim and scrapes for the stock you are going to make.

HEAT oven to 400 degrees. Place all the trimmings and scrapes in a roasting pan and roast in the oven until they are golden brown and dry. When meat is done, add some water to the roasting pan and scrape the entire flavor off the bottom as you loosen the meat. Let stand for 10 minutes. Put the scrapes and liquid in a 2-gallon stockpot and fill with cold water up to the inside of the handles. Bring to a boil; turn down to simmer and skim all the fat off the top with a ladle. Simmer for 6 hours, making sure to skim the fat every 20 minute, so that you do not get cloudy stock. Strain stock through a china cap and set aside.

HEAT oven to 350 degrees. In a roasting pan, sear the cheeks on both sides until nicely browned. As each of the cheeks finishes browning, place them into container. Set aside for later. Add all the vegetables and cook until sweated. Add wine and reduce by half. Add the browned cheeks and beef stock to roasting pan. Cover with a lid and place in 350-degree oven for 3½ hours.

AFTER 3 hours, check cheeks with tongs. They should be soft like pot roast; if not, continue cooking. When finished, remove carefully from liquid and place on lined sheet tray to cool. Strain the cheek jus, saving the liquid and discarding all solids.

WHEN ready to serve, put cheek jus, cheeks, and Vegetable Mix in a sauté pan. Bring to boil and reduce until you achieve a nice sauce consistency, thick but not too thick. Serve with potatoes mashed with a little horseradish.

***Serves 10 - 12***

*Wine suggestion: Cabernet Sauvignon*

## For the Vegetable Mix

*2 large carrots, large dice*
*1 pint white pearl onions*
*salt and pepper to taste*

HEAT oven to 400 degrees. Toss carrots with salt and pepper and roast in oven until soft to the squeeze. Cut off root end of the pearl onions, blanch in hot water, and cool in an ice bath. Squeeze them out of their skins. Mix carrots and pearl onions together and set aside until ready to finish cheeks.

# Bread Puddin'

## Ingredients

*4 loaves sliced white bread*
*2 pounds semi-sweet chocolate, chopped*
*oil or butter to coat pan*
*Crème Brulée Base (recipe follows)*

## Preparation

HEAT oven to 325 degrees. Trim crusts off bread and cut each slice into 9 equal pieces (3 across and 3 down), keeping each loaf separate. Coat a 4-inch hotel pan with oil or butter. Layer the ingredients evenly, starting with the first batch of bread. Spread the chopped chocolate evenly for the 2nd layer, and follow with the second batch of bread. Pour the Crème Brulée Base over the top and press down gently to make sure everything is soaked up evenly.

POUR 2 inches of water in the bottom of a 6-inch hotel pan. Place the 4-inch hotel pan into this and cover with foil. Bake in 325-degree oven for approximately 3 hours, rotating pan at least once. When the bread pudding has a firm jiggle through the center, remove foil and let the top brown, about 10 minutes.

***Serves 24***

## For the Crème Brulée Base

*1 gallon heavy cream*
*3 cups granulated sugar*
*2 tablespoons vanilla extract, or 1 vanilla bean*
*30 egg yolks*

BRING cream, sugar and vanilla bean just to a boil and turn off heat. If using extract, add it when everything is cool. Slowly temper hot cream mix into the egg yolks, whisking very fast. Remove vanilla bean before pouring onto bread and chocolate.

# Mortimer's

## *Jon Mortimer, Owner/Executive Chef*
## *Shara Mortimer, Owner*

Jon Mortimer has become a culinary icon in Boise. Since opening Mortimer's in 2000, Jon has garnered nearly fifty national and local awards for dining excellence. He also serves as an adjunct professor to Boise State University School of Culinary Arts, hosts the weekly radio show *Radio Café* on KIDO 580AM and serves as the television chef on KBCI channel 2's *Tip of the Day*. He has also written a delightful cookbook, *The Idaho Table*, and is working on a second book. Mortimer's has received the *Award of Excellence* from the *Wine Spectator* from the first year the restaurant was open. One of the private dining rooms is located in the wine cellar, which can hold up to 2,500 bottles.

Mortimer's is located below street level in the historic Belgravia Building in downtown Boise, and takes advantage of the rock structure of its interior. Built in 1904 out of rock quarried from Table Rock, the Belgravia was Boise's first elegant apartment building. Today, rough stone walls are set off by the crisp white linen tables and wait staff discreetly attired in black pants, white chef's jackets, and long gray aprons wrapped about the waist. Such touches add to the overall elegance of the dining experience. While Jon works his culinary magic in the kitchen, his wife, Shara, oversees the front of the house. She has trained the wait staff to be knowledgeable about the food and wine, and has trained them to be able to read their guests and tailor the service to their pleasure.

Chef Mortimer's culinary philosophy is deeply imbedded with his love of fresh, local ingredients, utilizing the bounty of the state of Idaho, from its trout-filled streams to its locally raised lamb and elk, as well as the many fine purveyors of produce in the Boise area. Born in Boston, but raised in Ketchum, Idaho, Jon got his start at a Ketchum steakhouse at the tender age of 14. After graduating from the University of Arizona, he attended the Horst Mager Culinary Academy, followed by forays to Norway, France, Italy, Denmark, Switzerland, and England that broadened his culinary experience and helped cultivate his own style of melding regional product with international influence. Returning stateside, he spent several years opening restaurants for companies including McCormick and Scmick's, but he and Shara longed for sunnier climes, moving to Boise in 1991.

# Crisp Polenta

*with Roasted Peppers and Mozzarella*

## Ingredients

- 2 *quarts chicken stock*
- 1 *teaspoon ground cumin*
- ½ *teaspoon cayenne pepper*
- *salt to taste*
- ½ *cup coarse ground corn meal, plus additional for dusting*
- 1½ *cups fine ground corn meal*
- 1 *cup grated mozzarella cheese*
- 1 *tablespoon fresh basil leaves, very fine julienne*
- 1 *roasted red pepper, seeded, stemmed, and julienned*
- 1 *quart canola oil*
- *Smoked Tomato Sauce (recipe follows)*
- *fresh basil leaves for garnish*

## Preparation

BRING the stock, cumin, cayenne and salt to a boil. Combine the two corn meals and slowly pour into the boiling stock in a steady stream while stirring constantly with a wooden polenta spoon or a stiff whisk. Be sure to add the polenta slowly and stir vigorously to avoid lumps. Lower heat and continue to cook and stir for an additional three minutes. Check the salt level one last time and remove from the heat.

BRUSH muffins tins with oil and dust with cornmeal. Fill them with half the prepared corn meal. Distribute the mozzarella, basil, and roasted peppers on top of the polenta in the muffin tins and cover with the remaining polenta. Pack it firm with a spoon. Set the polenta aside to cool completely, about 2 hours.

HEAT the canola oil in a large, thick skillet to about 350 degrees. If it is smoking then it is too hot; if you place the polenta in the pan it should immediately sizzle. Coat the prepared stuffed polentas with the extra corn meal and carefully place in the hot oil.

COOK for 1 minute, or until they start to brown, then carefully flip them over and repeat the process. Remove them from the pan and place them on a cooling rack to allow any excess oil to drain. If needed, they may be held in a warm oven for up to 5 minutes.

TO SERVE, center 1ounce of Smoked Tomato Sauce on a warmed plate. Place a piece of the polenta on top of the sauce and garnish with basil leaves.

## For the Smoked Tomato Sauce

- 4 *ripe red tomatoes*
- 1 *tablespoon olive oil*
- 4 *fresh basil leaves*
- 1 *tablespoon roasted garlic*
- 2 *tablespoons tomato paste*
- ½ *teaspoon ground black pepper*
- *kosher salt to taste*

CUT tomatoes in half, season and smoke. Heat the oil in a saucepan over medium heat and sauté the ingredients, stirring frequently. Blend ingredients until smooth.

***Serves 8***

# Dried Fruit Stuffed Chicken

*with Hibiscus Sauce*

## Ingredients

- *4 chicken breasts, skin on and short wing attached*
- *¼ cup dried pineapple, julienned*
- *¼ cup dried apricots, julienned*
- *¼ cup dried cranberries, julienned*
- *1 cup spinach leaves, julienned*
- *salt to taste*
- *ground black pepper to taste*
- *2 tablespoons melted butter*
- *4 sheets foil*
- *Hibiscus Sauce (recipe follows)*

## Preparation

HEAT grill to medium high heat. Slit a pocket laterally in each chicken breast. Combine the dried fruits and spinach in a bowl. Stuff the mixture into the chicken breasts and season with salt and pepper, coat with the melted butter and wrap in sheets of foil. Place the chicken breasts on the low rack of the grill and cook for about 1 minute on each side. Place the chicken on the high rack of the grill, slightly reduce the heat, and cook for 15 minutes. Place the chicken in the foil wraps on a cutting board and let rest for 5 minutes before carving.

TO SERVE, unwrap the chicken from the foil and place on a cutting board. Carve the chicken on a bias with a sharp knife. Place a large spoonful of Hibiscus Sauce on a plate and fan the carved chicken over the sauce.

***Serves 4***

*Wine suggestion: Adelsheim Vineyards 2004 Willamette Valley Pinot Noir*

## For the Hibiscus Sauce

- *3 tablespoons white vinegar*
- *2 teaspoons sugar*
- *2 cups roasted chicken stock*
- *¼ cup dried hibiscus petals*
- *1 tablespoon cornstarch dissolved in 2 tablespoons water*
- *kosher salt to taste*

IN A non-reactive saucepan bring the vinegar and the sugar to a boil. Cook the mixture until the sugar begins to caramelize. Add the stock to the mixture quickly so that the caramel does not burn, then add the hibiscus flowers to the pan and bring to a low boil. Allow the mixture to reduce by half, then whisk in the cornstarch with the mixture still at a low boil. Season the sauce to taste with the salt, then strain the sauce through a chinois or fine sauce strainer.

# Kobe Beef Kalbi

*with Tomato Rosemary Stew*

We get delicious Kobe Beef from Snake River Farms, right here in Idaho. If your butcher is not familiar with the term "kalbi", it is essentially boneless rib meat.

## Ingredients

- *24 ounces Snake River Farms Kobe beef kalbi*
- *ground black pepper*
- *ground sea salt, to taste*
- *1 teaspoon canola oil*
- *3 Yukon Gold potatoes, cooked and quartered*
- *¼ yellow onion, diced fine*
- *2 teaspoons roasted garlic purée*
- *1 teaspoon fresh rosemary leaves, chopped very fine*
- *¼ cup celery, bias sliced*
- *½ cup chopped tomato*
- *½ cup carrots, ornately chopped*
- *½ cup zucchini or yellow squash, ornately chopped*
- *1 tablespoon white wine vinegar*
- *½ cup dry white wine*
- *½ cup V-8 juice*
- *2 tablespoons heavy cream*
- *6 rosemary sprigs, for garnish*

## Preparation

SHAVE the kalbi into very thin strips and season lightly with the salt and pepper. Heat the oil in a skillet to just below the smoke point and sear the beef quickly and completely on both sides. Remove the beef from the pan and place it on a plate to keep warm while completing the rest of the dish.

PLACE the potatoes in the pan, frying them until they are golden brown. Put them on the plate with the meat. Reduce the heat on the pan to medium high and add the onion, stirring frequently until translucent. Add the roasted garlic, rosemary, and remaining vegetables to the pan and continue to cook for 3 to 4 minutes. Deglaze the pan with the vinegar and wine. After the liquid is reduced by half, add the tomato juice and return the potatoes to the pan. Allow to cook for 3 to 4 minutes, then whisk in the heavy cream and season to taste with salt and black pepper.

TO SERVE, take 6 large, warm pasta bowls and spoon the potato mixture into a pile in the center, then ladle several ounces of the broth over them. Garnish with the strips of meat and a rosemary sprig.

***Serves 6***

# Flat Iron Steak
*with Potato and Mushroom Fricassee*

## Ingredients

*46-ounce flat iron steaks*
*salt and black pepper to taste*
*Potato and Mushroom Fricassee (recipe follows)*

## Preparation

SEASON the steaks with salt and pepper and place on a well-seasoned grill. Cook to guests desired specifications, then place on a cutting board to rest for 2 minutes before slicing on a bias against the grain.

TO SERVE, ladle about ½ cup of the Potato and Mushroom Fricassee in the center of each warm entrée plate, then fan out the sliced pieces of the meat over it.

***Serves 4***

*Wine suggestion: Hell's Canyon "Reserve" Merlot, 2003*

## For the Potato and Mushroom Fricassee

*1 tablespoon canola oil*
*4 Yukon Gold potatoes, cooked and quartered*
*½ cup dry sherry*
*1 cup heavy cream*
*1 tablespoon Dijon mustard*
*1 tablespoon leek, white part only, sliced*
*1 red bell pepper, roasted, peeled and julienned*
*½ cup wild mushrooms, sliced - porcini, chanterelle, morel or any available*
*½ teaspoon ground black pepper*
*kosher salt to taste*

IN A sauté pan, heat the canola oil over medium-high heat, and then add the potatoes. Cook until brown on each side before turning. Repeat until brown on all sides. In a thick-bottomed saucepan combine the remaining ingredients and cook over medium heat for 30 minutes, or until the liquid is reduced by half. Drain any excess oil from the potatoes then add them to the saucepan and cook for 2 more minutes.

# Chandler's Restaurant

| Chandler's Restaurant | Baci Italian Café |
| --- | --- |
| 200 South Main Street | 240 South Main Street |
| Ketchum, ID 83340 | Ketchum, ID 83340 |
| 208-726-1776 | 208-726-8384 |
| www.chandlersrestaurant.com | www.chandlersrestaurant.com |
| Dinner nightly from 6:00pm | Dinner nightly from 6:00pm |

# Chandler's Restaurant

***Rex Chandler, Owner***
***Keith Otter, Executive Chef***

Nestled along picturesque Trail Creek on the south side of Ketchum sits a charming frame house set under huge old evergreens. Under Rex Chandler's supervision, it has been transformed into an elegant yet casual fine dining establishment. In the winter, enjoy dining in the cozy, intimate interior. As the weather warms, your dining options increase with the beautiful multi-level deck. As inside, you will enjoy white linen service, but can either dine under the stars, or under large canopies surrounded by lovely floral baskets and hanging lanterns.

In 1994, Rex Chandler decided to change his West Coast lifestyle that had him traveling between his restaurants in Newport Beach, California and Honolulu, Hawaii. He was looking for a healthy mountain atmosphere in a community that appreciated fine dining, a perfect description of the Sun Valley area. With him, he brought his brother-in-law, Keith Otter to serve as Executive Chef. Chef Otter is a graduate of the California Culinary Academy. He worked in San Francisco, serving as the sauté chef at Kuleto's and entremettier at Masa's under Julian Serrano. He also worked at Patina in West Hollywood, one of his brother-in-law's California establishments.

Chandler's features a sophisticated yet fun menu, featuring such Chef Specialties as Veal Ribeye on Black Truffle Risotto and "Nobu" Style Black Cod, as well as wonderful comfort foods such as Yankee Pot Roast and Idaho Black Canyon Elk Striploin with Potato-Parsnip Purée and Chokecherry-Huckleberry Chutney. The restaurant is also committed to maintaining a selection of wine that represents the best examples of New World wine-growing regions with an emphasis on Washington, Oregon, and California, as well as the wines of Italy, Spain, and Australia. The wines have been selected to pair well with the culinary offerings, and have resulted in Chandler's receiving the prestigious *Wine Spectator's Award of Excellence* for eight consecutive years.

After experiencing a delightful evening at Chandler's, you will want to enjoy another evening at Rex Chandler's other restaurant, right next door. Set in a historic cabin, Baci Italian Café and Wine Bar offers a romantic yet upbeat atmosphere in which to enjoy fresh, handmade Mediterranean fare. Baci's chef, Brent Rathmussen is also a graduate of the California Culinary Academy. Working under Executive Chef Otter, Chef Rathmussen credits him for giving him the classical training and inspiration to become a chef.

# Baci's Grilled Radicchio

*with Pancetta, Goat Cheese, and Basil*

## Ingredients

*1 head of radicchio, cut into 6 wedges*
*6 slices pancetta*
*2 wooden skewers, soaked in cold water*
*Caesar Dressing (recipe follows)*
*Balsamic Glaze (recipe follows)*
*goat cheese, for garnish*
*basil chiffonade, for garnish*
*brunoise of tomato, for garnish*

## Preparation

HEAT grill to medium. Wrap each wedge of radicchio with a slice of pancetta. Put 3 pancetta-radicchio wedges on each skewer and lightly grill over medium heat until bacon is crisp on both sides.

TO SERVE, place about 2 ounces of Caesar Dressing in the middle of each plate. Remove radicchio-pancetta wedges from skewers and place 3 wedges on each plate. Drizzle Balsamic Glaze around the plate. Crumble goat cheese on radicchio, then sprinkle tomatoes and basil on top.

***Serves 2***

*Wine suggestions: Italian Trebbiano Lugana, Guigol Cote de Rhone, or a Pinot Noir from Oregon or California's Sonoma Valley*

## For the Caesar Dressing

*1 teaspoon garlic, minced*
*1 teaspoon mustard*
*4 filets of white anchovies*
*1 egg*
*1 ounce white balsamic vinegar*
*1 teaspoon lemon juice*
*3 ounces olive oil*

PLACE all ingredients, except olive oil, in a food processor and blend. While processor is on, slowly add oil until emulsified.

## For the Balsamic Glaze

*1 cup balsamic vinegar*
*1 cup sherry vinegar*
*1 teaspoon honey*
*salt and pepper to taste*

IN A small saucepot, reduce vinegars by about 80%. Stir in honey and season with salt and pepper.

# Chandler's Day Boat Scallops

*with Crispy Potato Cake, Chanterelle Mushrooms, & Citrus Black Truffle Sauce*

## Ingredients

*20 U-10 scallops*
*canola oil*
*fresh chanterelle mushrooms*
*Potato Cakes (recipe follows)*
*Citrus Black Truffle Sauce (recipe follows)*

## Preparation

SAUTÉ scallops in a large sauté pan on medium heat with a small amount of canola oil until both sides are golden brown.

TO SERVE, place a Potato Cake in the center of each plate, with some fresh chanterelle mushrooms on top. Arrange scallops around the plate and spoon Citrus Truffle Sauce on top of each scallop.

## For the Potato Cakes

*2 potatoes, skinned, cut in large cubes, and blanched*
*2 potatoes, skinned, cut in large cubes, blanched, and milled or mashed until smooth*
*2 green onions, diced*
*1 teaspoon garlic, chopped*
*½ cup cream*
*salt & white pepper to taste*
*1 cup flour*
*1 cup canola oil*

DICE the 2 blanched potatoes and set aside. Combine the 2 milled potatoes with the green onions, garlic, and cream. Season to taste with salt and pepper. Fold in the diced potatoes. Form mixture into 3-ounce potatoes cakes by placing a 3-inch pastry cutter down, filling it with the mixture, and then removing the cutter. Dust each cake with flour. In a medium saucepan, add canola oil and heat over medium heat. Pan-fry the cakes until golden brown. Lightly season with salt and pepper and set aside.

## For the Citrus Truffle Sauce

*1 tablespoon shallots, chopped*
*2 cups vegetable stock*
*½ pound butter*
*salt and white pepper to taste*
*1 tablespoon black truffle purée or sliced truffle*
*¼ teaspoon truffle oil*
*1 teaspoon lemon juice*

COMBINE shallots and stock in a small saucepan, bring to a simmer and reduce by half. Blend in the butter and season with salt and pepper. Set aside in a warm spot. Just before serving, reheat and ad the truffle purée, truffle oil, and lemon juice.

***Serves 4 to 5***

*Wine suggestions: Flowers Pinot Noir, Sonoma Coast or Kistler Chardonnay*

# Baci's Roasted Sea Bass on Caramelized Fennel

*with Butter Sauce and Orange Vinaigrette*

## Ingredients

- 2 6-ounce portions sea bass
- salt & white pepper to taste
- olive oil for cooking
- 1 fennel bulb, sliced ⅛-inch
- 1 red onion, sliced ⅛-inch
- 3 cloves garlic, sliced
- 2 green olives, sliced
- 12 green beans, blanched and chilled
- 12 cherry tomatoes
- Butter Sauce (recipe follows)
- Orange Vinaigrette (recipe follows)

## Preparation

SEASON sea bass with salt and white pepper. In a pan heated over medium heat, sear sea bass on both sides with a small amount of olive oil, until golden brown. Set aside.

IN ANOTHER pan heated to medium heat, caramelize fennel slices in olive oil. Add slices of red onion, garlic, green olives, green beans, and cherry tomatoes. Season to taste with salt and pepper. When vegetables are tender, deglaze with Butter Sauce and 2 ounces of Orange Vinaigrette.

REHEAT sea bass for 2-3 minutes while plating the vegetables. Place the heated sea bass on the vegetables and serve.

***Serves 2***

*Wine suggestions: a Pinot Noir, or Harford Chardonnay, or Chianti Frescabaldi*

## For the Butter Sauce

- 1 ounce shallots, chopped
- 1 teaspoon garlic, minced
- 2 cups chicken stock
- 4 ounces butter
- salt and white pepper to taste

COMBINE shallots, garlic and stock in small saucepan. Bring to a simmer and reduce by half. Blend in the butter and season to taste with salt and pepper. Keep warm.

## For the Orange Vinaigrette

- 2 ounces red wine vinegar
- 2 ounces sherry vinegar
- 1 teaspoon garlic, minced
- 2 ounces shallots, chopped
- 1 teaspoon fresh thyme, finely chopped
- 1 teaspoon orange zest, finely chopped
- salt and pepper
- 12 ounces Pommace olive oil

IN A bowl, combine the vinegars, garlic, shallot, thyme, orange zest, and season with salt and pepper. Slowly whisk in olive oil and set aside. ***Yield: about 2 cups***

# Baci's Lamb Ragu

*with Winter Root Vegetables on Fusilli Pasta & Red Wine Sauce*

## Ingredients

- *4 lamb shanks*
- *salt & pepper*
- *2 cups flour*
- *2 cups canola oil*
- *1 onion, chopped*
- *3 celery stalks, chopped*
- *3 carrots, chopped*
- *3 cloves garlic,*
- *½ cup tomato paste*
- *3 cups red wine*
- *4 cups veal stock*
- *2 cups chicken stock*
- *1 sprig fresh thyme*
- *3 bay leaves*
- *6 black peppercorns*
- *1 orange peel and juice*
- *Winter Root Vegetables (recipe follows)*
- *1 ounce butter*
- *1 pound fusilli pasta, blanched until almost al denté & coated in olive oil*
- *Gremolata (recipe follows)*
- *Grated fresh Parmesan, for garnish*

## Preparation

HEAT oven to 450 degrees. Season lamb shanks with salt and pepper, then dredge each shank into flour. In a large sauté pan, heat canola oil on medium heat and slowly pan-fry each shank until golden brown on all sides. Remove shanks and place into a deep baking dish and set aside.

SAUTÉ onions, celery, carrots, and garlic on medium heat until vegetables are lightly caramelized. Stir in tomato paste and continue to cook until vegetables are well coated. Deglaze with red wine. Bring to a boil and pour mixture over lamb shanks. Add veal stock and chicken stock to cover the shanks completely. Add thyme sprig, bay leaves, peppercorns, and orange peel with juice. Cover with foil and bake in 450-degree oven for 3 hours until lamb falls from bone. Remove from oven and let cool. Pull meat from bones and place in a separate container. Discard bones and strain the braising liquid into a saucepan and reduce by half.

SAUTÉ the pulled lamb in a large pan with salt and pepper, and then add Winter Vegetables. Sauté until mixture is hot and deglaze with the reduced braising liquid. Add the butter and toss in cooked fusilli pasta. Continue to cook mixture for 1 minute.

SERVE in a large bowl garnished with freshly grated Parmesan. Sprinkle Gremolata on top.

***Serves 6 to 8***

*Wine suggestion: Vino Avignonese Nobile de Montepulciano*

## For the Winter Root Vegetables

*1 onion*
*3 stalks celery*
*2 carrots*
*1 butternut squash*
*3 cloves garlic*
*olive oil*
*salt and pepper to taste*

MEDIUM dice the onion, celery, carrots, squash, and finely chop the garlic. In a sauté pan, lightly sauté vegetables in olive oil until vegetables are soft. Season with salt and pepper and set aside.

## For the Gremolata

*1 teaspoon orange zest*
*1 tablespoon pine nuts, toasted*
*1 sprig fresh thyme*
*1 sprig fresh rosemary*
*1 sprig fresh parsley*

FINELY chop each ingredient separately and then combine together. Set aside.

# Chandler's 'Nobu' Style Black Cod

*with Jasmine Rice in a Gingered Broth*

## Ingredients

*1 black cod filet, skin on – enough to serve 5 to 6*
*Sake-Miso Marinade (recipes follows)*
*Gingered Broth (recipe follows)*
*Jasmine Rice (recipe follows)*

## Preparation

PLACE cod filet in Sake-Miso Marinade in refrigerator for 24 hours, turning to be sure both sides are marinated.

WHEN ready to cook, heat oven to 450 degrees. Cut filet into 5 or 6 individual portions, cutting the rib bones completely out. Oven broil cod filets for 8-10 minutes or until golden brown.

TO SERVE, place Jasmine Rice in individual serving bowls. Place cod filet on top of rice and pour hot Gingered Broth around. Spoon vegetables and shrimp on last.

***Serves 5 to 6***

*Wine suggestions: something with a good acidity, such as a German Riesling or Gëwurztraminer, or an Oregon Pinto Noir*

### For the Sake-Miso Marinade

*1 cup white miso paste*
*½ cup sake*
*½ cup sugar*
*1 tablespoon soy sauce*

THOROUGHLY combine all ingredients.

### For the Gingered Broth

*1 cup rice wine vinegar*
*6 cups chicken stock (canned broth is fine)*
*1 tablespoon fresh ginger, diced*
*4 green onions (white part only), sliced*
*1 carrot, thinly sliced*
*1 cup rock shrimp*
*1 cup shiitake mushrooms, sliced*
*½ cup cilantro, chopped*
*1 teaspoon lemon grass, finely chopped*
*¼ cup white soy sauce (optional)*

PLACE all ingredients in a saucepan. Bring to a boil right before serving.

### For the Jasmine Rice

*2 cups jasmine rice*
*4 cups water*

SCRUB the rice with cold water. Place the cleaned rice in a pot with the 4 cups of water. Cover, and steam for 12-15 minutes.

# *Felix's Restaurant*

P.O. Box 476
380 First Ave. North
Ketchum, ID 83340
208-726-1166

Open for dinner 7 nights a week at 6:00 pm
Tapas Night:
Wednesday - open at 5:00 pm
Closed for 5 weeks in April & early May

# Felix's Restaurant

### *Felix Gonzalez, Chef and Owner*

The small log house tucked under huge old pine trees in downtown Ketchum seems to exude a warm welcome to you as you pass through the wrought iron fence that surrounds Felix's Restaurant. The exterior logs are stained a soft sage green and are set off perfectly by the deep red welcoming door and shutters. On pleasant summer evenings, diners can enjoy their meals outside on the patio surrounding the house, with large white awnings to protect against the occasional mountain shower. Inside, diners are seated at comfortable leather chairs and treated to crisp white linen tablecloths in the warm setting of this lovely old home.

Felix Gonzalez emigrated with his family to Ketchum from his native Spain at the age of 18. Felix's culinary talents are self-taught and were first ignited by his love of his mother's cooking. He credits her for his love of fine food and his simple cooking style. Felix honed his gastronomic skills by spending many years working in some of Sun Valley's finer restaurants. In 1992 he opened Felix's Restaurant, and eight years later, moved the restaurant to its present location. The log house was originally his parent's home where they lived for 35 years. Felix has converted the residence into a quaint and personable restaurant that seats 50 guests in the winter and 100 guests during the warm summer months when garden dining is a popular alternative.

During those warm summer months, Felix features a Tapas Night in the garden. Here, guests are treated to a Spanish wine flight and small appetizers to share. Many locals enjoy this before moving on to entertainment in the area, or before enjoying a leisurely full-course dinner at Felix's.

Felix's culinary style is best described as continental, with a Mediterranean flair. His Basque heritage shines through in the house's signature dish: Felix's Braised Lamb Shanks. Although it is not always on the menu, locals often call ahead to order this exceptional dish. Nightly specials feature the season's best offerings enhanced by Felix's special culinary genius. The large wine cellar specializes in Spanish and American wines, and the competent wait staff is more than happy to help you with your wine selections, as well as a variety of beers. An evening at Felix's Restaurant is truly a unique Sun Valley experience.

# Calamari Picante

This tapa or appetizer has been on our menu since we opened in 1992 and no one ever gets tired of it. Some guests order it entrée size. "The best calamari I've ever eaten" usually follows!

## Ingredients

*calamari steaks*
*flour*
*salt*
*olive oil*
*tomatoes, diced and seeds removed*
*green onions, diced*
*shallots, diced*
*garlic, finely chopped*
*parsley, chopped*
*fresh thyme*
*dried red chili peppers to taste*
*lemon juice to taste*

## Preparation

CUT the calamari into strips and dust lightly with flour and salt. Prepare the tomatoes, green onions, shallots, garlic, parsley, and thyme, allowing 1 teaspoon of each per serving.

IN A skillet, heat olive oil and flash-fry the calamari strips to a golden brown. Do not overcook, as this will toughen the strips. Add the tomatoes, green onions, shallots, garlic, parsley, and thyme to the skillet along with a dash of salt. Add dried red chili peppers to taste and squeeze several drops of lemon juice over all, stirring to combine. Serve immediately.

*Wine suggestion: A Morgadio Albarino, a full-bodied Spanish white wine from the Rias Baixas, or a Lan Reserva Spanish red from the Rioja region.*

# Spanish Tortilla with Ensalada Andaluza

## Ingredients

- ¼ *cup olive oil*
- ¼ *cup salad oil*
- 6 *large Idaho potatoes, peeled & cut in ⅛-inch slices*
- 1 *large onion, thinly sliced*
- 6 *large eggs*
- *salt to taste*
- *Ensalada Andaluza (recipe follows)*

## Preparation

HEAT the oil in a 9-inch skillet. Add potato slices slowly, alternating with onion slices, and salt each layer lightly. Cook slowly over a medium flame until tender, but not brown.

IN A large bowl, beat the eggs with a fork until they are slightly foamy, and add salt to taste. Remove potato-onion mixture from the skillet and drain, reserving 3 tablespoons of the oil. Add the potato mixture to the beaten eggs, pressing the potatoes down so that the eggs cover them. Let the mixture sit for 15 minutes.

HEAT 2 tablespoons of the reserved oil in a large skillet until very hot. Add the potato and egg mixture, spreading it out in the skillet. Lower the heat and, when the potatoes begin to brown on the bottom, invert a plate of the same size over the skillet. Flip the omelet onto the plate. Add a little more oil to the skillet, and slide the omelet back into the skillet to brown the other side. If your skillet is not hot enough, the omelet may stick to the pan. The tortilla should be a little juicy in the middle and should hold the shape of the skillet. Transfer to a plate and let stand for 15 minutes.

SERVE the tortilla at room temperature with the Ensalada Andaluza as described below.

***Serves 8 – 10 as an appetizer***

## For the Ensalada Andaluza

- 1 *can or bottle roasted red peppers*
- *olive oil*
- 1 *clove garlic, minced*
- *chopped parsley*
- 1 *bag mixed greens*
- 1 *pound Spanish Manchego cheese, sliced ⅛-inch thick in a pie shape*
- 24-30 *slices Spanish chorizo, pre-cooked*
- 30-40 *Spanish olives*

RINSE the red peppers and slice into strips. Add a dash of olive oil, the garlic, and parsley, and toss to combine.

TO SERVE, place a serving of mixed greens on each plate. Slice the Spanish Tortilla as you would a pie, to allow a slice or two per serving. Surround the mixed greens with the sliced tortilla, 2 slices of Manchego cheese, and 3 slices of Spanish chorizo. Put the red pepper mixture in the middle on top of the greens and garnish each plate with 4 or 5 Spanish olives.

# Merluza a la Vasca

Serve this dish with boiled potatoes and a green salad.

## Ingredients

- 4 *fish steaks, such as fresh cod, preferably about 1 inch thick*
- ½ *cup flour, divided*
- *salt and pepper to taste*
- 4 *tablespoons olive oil, divided*
- 4 *teaspoons lemon juice*
- 4 *garlic cloves, minced*
- 3 *tablespoons onion, minced*
- ¾ *cup white wine*
- ¾ *cup clam juice*
- 9 *tablespoons parsley, minced and divided*
- ¾ *cup fresh or frozen peas*
- 12 *clams*
- 12 *mussels*
- 2 *hard-boiled eggs, finely chopped*

## Preparation

HEAT oven to 350 degrees. Sprinkle fish steaks with salt and pepper. Reserve 2 tablespoons of the flour, and use the rest to lightly dust the fish. Heat 2 tablespoons of the olive oil in a skillet, and sauté the fish steaks 1 minute on each side. Put each steak in an individual oven-proof dish and sprinkle each with 1 teaspoon lemon juice.

CLEAN skillet with a paper towel, add 2 more tablespoons olive oil, and sauté the garlic and onion. Stir in the reserved 2 tablespoons of flour, and gradually pour in the wine and clam juice. Stir until the sauce is thickened and smooth. Add 5 tablespoons of the parsley, the peas, and salt and pepper to taste. Pour equal amounts of the sauce over each steak. Decorate each dish with 3 clams and 3 mussels. Their juices and flavor to the sauce.

PLACE dishes in 350-degree oven and bake for 15-20 minutes, or until the fish flakes and the shellfish open. Discard any shellfish that fail to open. Sprinkle each dish with the chopped eggs and the remaining parsley and serve.

***Serves 4***

*Wine suggestion: An Albarino white wine or a chardonnay.*

# Felix's Braised Lamb Shanks

Felix's Basque and Spanish heritage has naturally made lamb his signature dish. It is not always on our menu, but guests will call ahead to order, as it has become a favorite among our loyal clients.

## Ingredients

*4 lamb shanks*
*salt and coarse black pepper*
*fresh thyme, chopped*
*fresh rosemary, chopped*
*olive oil*
*1 white onion, rough chopped*
*1 carrot, rough chopped*
*1 celery rib, rough chopped*
*1 medium potato, peeled & rough chopped*
*4 cloves garlic, chopped*
*½ cup flour*
*1 quart chicken stock*
*1 bottle white wine*
*balsamic vinegar to taste*

## Preparation

HEAT oven to 400 degrees. Trim as much fat and silver from the lamb shanks as possible, leaving meat intact. Season shanks with salt, pepper, thyme, and rosemary. In a heavy metal roasting pan, brown the shanks in olive oil. When shanks are browned half way, add the onion, carrot, celery, potato, and garlic. Caramelize all vegetables, stirring often, until golden brown.

STRAIN fat from vegetables and shanks. Dust with flour, stirring mixture and cooking until it thickens. Add chicken stock (preferably homemade) and white wine. Put in oven 400-degree oven, uncovered, for 2-3 hours.

WHEN shanks are done (the meat is ready to fall off the bone), remove them from the sauce. Purée all of the vegetables and sauce together. Strain through a fine sieve, taste for seasoning, and add balsamic vinegar to taste. Serve shanks with the sauce.

***Serves 4***

*Wine suggestion: A great Spanish red wine, such as Pasanau la Planeta, a full-bodied expressive red wine from the Priorat region, or Condado de Haza from the Ribera del Duero region.*

# Abuela's Spanish Flan

## Ingredients

*16 tablespoons sugar, divided*
*5 teaspoons water*
*3 whole eggs*
*3 egg yolks*
*¼ teaspoon orange rind, grated*
*2½ cups milk*
*freshly picked pansies, for garnish*

## Preparation

HEAT oven to 350 degrees. To caramelize the sugar, combine 10 tablespoons of sugar and 5 teaspoons of water in a small skillet over medium heat. Stir constantly until sugar turns a golden color. Remove from heat and pour into 6 ovenproof custard cups.

WITH a wire whisk, beat the whole eggs and egg yolks. Add grated orange rind, the remaining 6 tablespoons of sugar, and the milk, whisking to combine. Pour into the caramelized cups. Place the filled cups in a pan of hot water and cook on top of stove over medium heat for 1 hour. Transfer the pan and cups to 350-degree oven and cook for an additional 25 minutes. The flans are done when a knife inserted into the custard comes out clean. Remove the custard cups from the water and cool, then refrigerate.

TO SERVE, loosen the custard with a knife, going around the edge of each cup. Invert onto dessert plates and garnish with a pansy, if desired.

***Serves 6***

*The Horace C. Lewis residence. Ketchum, Idaho ca. 1885*

# Ketchum Grill

520 East Ave.
Ketchum, ID 83340
208-726-4660
www.ketchumgrill.com

Dinner:
5:30 pm nightly

# Ketchum Grill

### *Scott Mason, Owner and Chef*

Sitting at the north edge of town on East Avenue, between 5th and 6th Streets is a lovely old wood frame building that is the home of the Ketchum Grill. Built around 1885, the building served as a residence until the early 70s, when it was converted into a restaurant. The beautiful clear fir floors of the original residence were preserved, lending special warmth. Recently the wooden front porch was replaced with a brick patio that is covered by a canvas awning for summer seating.

Chef and owner, Scott Mason, grew up in Eugene, Oregon, where he began learning about the culinary world from his grandmother. He would help with the family breakfasts aided by a cast iron skillet and a step stool. After four years of college and working at several Eugene restaurants, Scott ventured south to Santa Barbara to continue his education. However, his love of the food world won out, and Scott obtained a pantry position at Norbert's, as well as landing a job in the kitchen at San Ysidro Ranch. At the Ranch, Scott met his future wife, Anne, who was employed as the Pastry Chef. Scott moved up to take over the position of Sous Chef at Norbert's and recruited Anne to join him there as their Pastry Chef. The two helped Norbert open two other restaurants in three years. To enhance their culinary repertoire, Scott and Anne took a 3-month sabbatical and toured the restaurants and markets of Europe. Upon their return, Scott took the position of Chef at Alessia Restaurant in Marin County, adding a strong knowledge of Italian cooking to his background.

After a couple of years in the Bay Area, Scott, Anne, and their first child decided to move to the less hectic lifestyle of the mountains of central Idaho. Scott obtained a position at Freddy's Tavern D'Alsace, the restaurant that preceded the Ketchum Grill in the building on East Avenue. At Freddy's, Scott began experimenting with making his own sausages and pâtés. Noting Scott's passion for food, the owner of Freddy's arranged for Scott to apprentice at four French/Alsatian restaurants in Paris and Alsace. This reaffirmed Scott's knowledge of French cuisine and enhanced his techniques.

In 1991, back in Ketchum, Scott had the opportunity to fulfill the dream of owning a restaurant, by purchasing Freddy's and making it his own as the Ketchum Grill. Today, the Ketchum Grill attracts celebrities, foodies, and locals with its classic dishes enhanced by seasonal, fresh ingredients and reasonable prices. An extensive wine list includes a wide variety of California wines, supplemented by a nice selection of Northwestern wines, as well as some international selections

# Grilled Chanterelle and Roasted Vegetable Pizza

This recipe can also be served as 1 large pizza.

## Ingredients

- 6 *pizza doughs, par cooked*
- 2 *pounds chanterelle mushrooms, cut in large slices*
- 1 *cup virgin olive oil, divided*
- 2 *teaspoons garlic, chopped & divided*
- 1 *pinch kosher salt*
- 1 *pinch secret herbs (equal parts dry sage, thyme, & oregano)*
- 1 *zucchini, cut in ¼ inch strips*
- 1 *yellow onion, cut in ¼ inch strips*
- 2 *fennel bulbs, cut in ¼ inch strips*
- 3 *cups tomato, peeled, seeded, & diced*
- ½ *pound Asiago cheese, grated*

## Preparation

HEAT oven to 400 degrees. Place chanterelle mushrooms into a mixing bowl with ¼ cup of the olive oil, 1 teaspoon garlic, kosher salt and a pinch of secret herbs. Toss to coat and set aside.

PLACE zucchini, onion, and fennel in an ovenproof pan and toss with 2 tablespoons of olive oil, the remaining garlic, and a pinch of salt. Roast in 400-degree oven for 30 minutes. Remove vegetables and raise oven heat to 550 degrees.

MEANWHILE, on a grill set over medium fire, cook chanterelle mushrooms for about 5 minutes. Take caution of flare ups and be careful not to turn the mushrooms too much or they may fall between the spaces in the grill. Remove the chanterelle to a clean container.

PLACE pizza doughs on a baking sheet, or on a flat surface if you are using an oven pizza stone. Make sure that tomatoes are well drained. Brush doughs with remaining olive oil and arrange tomatoes on each round. Add the grilled vegetables and chanterelles and sprinkle lightly with grated cheese. Bake for 10 minutes in a 550-degree oven. Remove and cut into 6 or 8 pieces with a pizza cutter or a chef's knife. Serve hot.

***Serves 6 – 8 as an appetizer***

# LINGUINE WITH GRILLED QUAIL, MUSTARD, HERBS, AND DRIED TOMATOES

This pasta has been on our menu for nearly 14 years. Aside from being one of the Ketchum Grill's signature menu items, this dish remains one of my most requested recipes. The recipe itself is very easy to make and anyone who can boil water should be able to make a consistent and flavorful pasta meal.

## Ingredients

- ⅓ *cup Dijon mustard*
- 1 *teaspoon garlic, minced*
- ¼ *cup sun dried tomatoes (softened in warm water)*
- 12 *Kalamata olives*
- 1 *tablespoon fresh rosemary, chopped*
- 1 *tablespoon fresh thyme, chopped*
- 2 *tablespoons chopped fresh parsley*
- 2 *cups chicken stock (preferably homemade or low salt)*
- ½ *cup heavy cream (optional)*
- 1½ *pounds dry linguine pasta, cooked to al dente & drained*
- *Grilled Quail (recipe follows)*
- ½ *cup Parmesan cheese, freshly grated*

## Preparation

COMBINE the mustard, garlic, tomatoes, olives, herbs, chicken stock, and optional cream in a large sauté pan and bring to a boil. Add cooked pasta, and toss together. Heat sauce and pasta until boiling and desired consistency is reached. If the pasta seems a little too dry, add a touch more stock. If the sauce seems a little too thin, cook off some of the liquid. (We serve the sauce on the thinner side at the Ketchum Grill.)

WITH tongs, remove pasta from sauce and divide between 6 serving plates or into one large serving bowl. Pour remaining sauce over the top. Serve hot pasta with the Grilled Quail arranged on top and sprinkled with freshly grated Parmesan cheese.

## For the Grilled Quail

- 6 *quail, semi-boneless*
- 1 *pinch Kosher salt*
- 1 *tablespoon fresh rosemary, chopped*
- 2 *tablespoons olive oil, if cooking in a pan*

THE quail we use at The Grill is a sleeve boned or semi-boneless quail. Season each quail on both sides with salt and rosemary. In a hot pan, or over hot coals, cook the quail to medium.

REMOVE from heat and arrange quail on top of linguine.

***Serves 6 as an appetizer***

# Oven Roasted Beet Salad

## Ingredients

*10 large red beets, peeled and sliced*
*olive oil*
*1 pinch kosher salt*
*1 cup honey*
*2 cups balsamic vinegar*
*2 pounds spinach, cleaned*
*½ cup goat cheese*
*¼ cup walnuts, toasted*

## Preparation

HEAT oven to 400 degrees. Place beets in a roasting pan, toss with olive oil, and roast for 45 minutes or until tender. Warm honey and balsamic vinegar together in a saucepot and toss with warm beets. Place beets on a bed of spinach and top with crumbled goat cheese and toasted walnuts. For a variation, try using spiced walnuts.

***Serves 6***

*Suggested wine: A crisp Alsatian Riesling or Pinot Gris*

# Wild Mushroom Strudel with Port Wine Sauce

If chanterelle mushrooms are not available, you can substitute fresh cepes, shaggy manes, or morels. Even domestic mushrooms will work for this recipe. The Port Wine Sauce we make at the Ketchum Grill is a by-product of our Lamb Shanks. The recipe here is similar and can be prepared without the labor of cooking lamb shanks first.

## Ingredients

- *½ pound unsalted butter, divided*
- *1 yellow onion, diced*
- *2 pounds chanterelle mushrooms, washed & cut*
- *2 pounds cream cheese*
- *1 pinch white pepper*
- *1 teaspoon Tabasco sauce*
- *1 teaspoon dried thyme*
- *1 pinch kosher salt*
- *10 sheets phyllo dough*
- *2 cups Japanese "Panko" bread crumbs*
- *Port Wine Sauce (recipe follows)*

## Preparation

HEAT oven to 400 degrees. In a large sauté pan melt 2 tablespoons of the butter and add diced onion. Cook onion until translucent and add mushrooms. Sauté mushrooms over medium heat until they begin to loose their liquid. Add the cream cheese, white pepper, Tabasco, and thyme. Continue to cook over medium heat while stirring the mushrooms to melt the cream cheese and to thoroughly mix in the seasonings. The mixture will be thin at first, but with continued cooking the cheese will melt and begin to tighten or thicken the filling. The filling is ready when it becomes thick like pudding and the cream cheese is completely melted with no lumps remaining. Check the seasoning and add salt if desired.

MELT the remaining butter. On a baking sheet, lay out 1 sheet of phyllo. Brush with melted butter and lay out another sheet on top. Repeat buttering and layering phyllo until all 10 sheets are used.

PLACE mushroom and cheese mixture on the middle of the layered phyllo from end to end in an even cylindrical shape. Fold 1 edge of the phyllo over the mushroom mixture and roll to surround mixture with phyllo while maintaining a long and cylindrical shape. With the seam side of the phyllo down, brush the top of strudel with melted butter and place sheet pan with strudel in 400-degree oven for 15 minutes or until golden brown. When done remove from oven and allow to cool.

TO SERVE, slice strudel into 1½ inch slices. Bread each exposed side with breadcrumbs and sauté in a Teflon pan with melted butter or olive oil until golden brown. To serve, ladle some of the Port Wine Sauce onto appetizer plates. Place the sliced strudel onto each plate and drizzle a small amount of the sauce over top. Serve hot with a salad of organic lettuces and raspberry vinaigrette.

***Serves 10***

### For the Port Wine Sauce

- 2 *cups port wine*
- 1 *shallot, diced*
- 1 *cup unsalted or lightly salted chicken stock*
- 4 *tablespoons tomato paste*
- ¼ *teaspoon paprika*
- 1 *teaspoon lemon juice*
- *fresh ground pepper*
- 4 *tablespoons unsalted butter*
- *salt to taste*

IN A small stainless saucepan, place the port and the shallot. Over medium heat, reduce liquid to 1 cup. Add stock, tomato paste, paprika, lemon juice and a few turns fresh ground pepper. Bring back to a boil and stir in the butter. Check for seasonings.

## Ketchum Grill Rosemary Raisin Bread

At the Grill we allow our bread dough to rise at least 24 hours. A longer rise will give a better flavor. If you have too much dough, it will keep, covered, in the refrigerator for up to a week.

### Ingredients

- 4½ *pounds bread flour*
- ½ *pound wheat flour, whole grain*
- ½ *cup golden raisins*
- 3 *tablespoons fresh rosemary, chopped*
- ¼ *cup kosher salt*
- 1 *tablespoon sugar*
- 2 *ounces dry yeast*
- 7½ *cups warm water*

### Preparation

PLACE flours, raisins, rosemary and salt in a large mixing bowl. Place the sugar and yeast in another bowl. Pour the warm water over yeast and sugar and whisk lightly. Allow the yeast to proof for 10 minutes. Pour proofed yeast over flour mixture and mix with hands or a heavy wooden spoon until stiff enough to knead. On a floured work surface knead bread for 10 minutes. Shape dough into a large ball, place in a large clean mixing bowl, and cover for at least 2 hours and up to 24 hours.

HEAT oven to 400 degrees. Cut the dough into 1½ pound pieces and shape into cylinders or rounds. Allow to rise again for about 30-45 minutes. Place in 400-degree oven and bake until golden to dark brown, depending on your preference. Allow to cool for 15 minutes (if you can) before cutting. Enjoy!

***Yield: 7 or 8 loaves***

# Ketchum Grill Rock Shrimp Cakes

## Ingredients

- 2 tablespoons unsalted butter
- 2 medium onions, minced
- 3 stalks celery, minced
- 2 tablespoons Tabasco
- 1 teaspoon white pepper, ground
- ¼ cup fresh dill, chopped
- 3 pounds cream cheese, at room temp
- 6 egg yolks
- 2 pounds rock shrimp, rinsed, drained, & coarsely chopped
- 4–5 cups Japanese breadcrumbs, divided

## Preparation

MELT butter in sauté pan. Sauté onion and celery until translucent. Add Tabasco, white pepper, and fresh dill. Mix together and set aside.

IN A mixer equipped with a paddle, cream together the cream cheese and egg yolks. Stir in celery and onions and add rock shrimp. Stir again until shrimp are incorporated with cheese. Reserve ½ cup of breadcrumbs and set aside. Add remaining crumbs to the shrimp to help bind the mixture. Place in refrigerator until thoroughly chilled, at least 30 minutes.

SCOOP and shape shrimp mixture into ½-inch thick silver dollar sized cakes. Pat remaining bread crumbs on outside of cakes to help keep them from sticking. Heat a sauté pan and add olive oil, followed by shrimp cakes. Do not crowd the cakes in the pan or they will be hard to flip. Brown on one side, flip, reduce heat and cook until heated through, about 5 minutes. Finished cakes can be held in a preheated oven while the others are cooking.

SERVE with a Remoulade, Tartar or Aioli Sauce. Cake batter can be prepared ahead and kept for two or three days in the refrigerator.

***Serves 10 – 12***

*Wine suggestion: A crisp Sancere*

# Lamb and Wild Rice Meatballs

You can serve these meatballs with a favorite sauce, on a salad, or as an excellent addition to spaghetti with marinara sauce. The Prairie Fire is a spice we make in our own kitchen in large amounts and use it as a seasoning for grilled meats and fish. We have broken it down into parts for home use in this recipe. You can probably use 1 tablespoon as equal to 1 part.

## Ingredients

- *1/3 cup milk*
- *2/3 cup cream*
- *1 cup Japanese breadcrumbs*
- *3 1/3 pounds lamb, ground*
- *1 yellow onion, diced fine*
- *1 cup wild rice, cooked*
- *1 egg*
- *2 2/3 tablespoons herbs de Provence*
- *1 1/3 tablespoons kosher salt*
- *1 tablespoon Prairie Fire (recipe follows)*
- *1 cup tomato juice*

## Preparation

HEAT oven to 350 degrees. Mix milk, cream, and breadcrumbs and allow to soak. Mix together with lamb, onions, rice, eggs, and seasonings. Shape into 2-ounce balls and brown in a hot skillet.

REMOVE to baking pan; add tomato juice and covered with a lid or foil. Bake in 350-degree oven for 30 minutes.

***Serves 10***

## For the Prairie Fire

- *2 parts paprika*
- *1 part cayenne*
- *1 part curry*
- *1 part dried thyme*
- *1 part chili powder*
- *1 part ground black pepper*
- *1 part anise seed*

COMBINE all ingredients. Store in a glass jar.

# Pan Seared Wild Mallard

*with Black Pepper, Soy and Orange*

## Ingredients

- 12 *wild duck breasts, boned & skinned*
- 4 *tablespoons olive oil*
- ½ *cup soy sauce*
- 2 *tablespoons honey*
- ½ *cup white wine*
- 2 *tablespoons fresh ginger root, peeled & julienned*
- 2 *oranges, zested & sectioned*
- 1 *tablespoon black pepper, coarsely crushed*
- 2 *pounds cleaned Asian Greens or Spinach*

## Preparation

HEAT large sauté pan and add olive oil followed by duck breasts. Cook 1-2 minutes over high heat; turn breasts and cook another 1-2 minutes. Add soy sauce, honey, wine, ginger, and orange zest, stirring to combine. Bring to a boil and cook duck breasts in liquid until done but still pink in the middle. Do not overcook. Remove duck from pan and arrange over a salad of Asian greens or spinach. Garnish with orange sections. Drizzle sauce over the top. Serve hot.

***Serves 6***

# The Roosevelt Tavern and Grille

280 N. Main
Ketchum, ID 83340
208-726-0051

Lunch & Dinner
Open daily: 11:45 am to 10:00 pm

# The Roosevelt Tavern and Grille

## Tom Nickel, Owner

A great place for a casual lunch or après ski beverage and appetizer, The Roosevelt Tavern and Grille also offers a varied dinner menu that will please the entire family. Located on the corner of Main Street and Sun Valley Road, the tavern sits on the plot of land where the Palace Hotel was built. When the Palace opened in 1885, it boasted Ketchum's finest lodging, as well as a dining room and bar. Later a man named Slavey Werry opened Slavey's, which had a colorful Ketchum history of burgers, beers, and bands. The rooftop of the restaurant offers additional outdoor dining, with large wood-fired pits to warm the cool nights and create a romantic atmosphere. The glass panels surrounding the deck ward off some of the wind, and let in the view of Baldy and the downtown streets of Ketchum.

The Roosevelt Tavern is named for the Roosevelt elk, a species of elk that was identified in 1897 and named after Theodore Roosevelt, who helped in the preservation of the elk and its habitats. A shoulder mount of a Roosevelt elk is the centerpiece of the dining room, mounted above the beautiful old oval bar.

The interior of the restaurant is large and open, sporting exposed brick walls and lots of dark wood. The walls are decorated with sporting gear covering the gamut of Sun Valley pursuits: fishing gear, skis, snowshoes, and even a sled. Old pictures of the Ketchum area and citizens, as well as vintage Sun Valley ads complete the wall décor.

As you walk into the tavern, you feel that you are stepping into a friendly neighborhood pub. In the fall of 2005, a large, beautiful fireplace was added. Leather couches and easy chairs surround the fireplace, making it a great spot to enjoy a glass of wine and an appetizer after skiing or before dinner. The food at the Roosevelt can best be described as eclectic American, covering everything from fresh-caught Idaho trout to southern jambalaya to juicy buffalo burgers. The wine list offers mainly California wines, with a sprinkling of Northwest selections, and the beer selection includes at least 10 on draught. One of the few places in Ketchum to serve cocktails at lunch, the tavern features a list of specialty drinks to suit all appetites.

# Smoked Idaho Trout and Artichoke Dip

## Ingredients

- ½ *cup sun-dried tomatoes*
- ½ *pound smoked Idaho trout, skin off*
- 2 *cups mayonnaise*
- 1½ *pounds cream cheese*
- 2 *cups Parmesan cheese, shredded*
- 1 *pound artichoke hearts, drained and chopped*
- ½ *tablespoon garlic, minced*
- ⅛ *cup olive oil*
- ½ *cup red onion, diced*
- *chopped chives, for garnish*
- *shredded Parmesan, for garnish*
- *toasted sourdough bread*

## Preparation

SOAK sun-dried tomatoes in warm water for 5 minutes. Mince the smoked trout in a food processor, and then put in a bowl. Mix in mayonnaise, cream cheese, and Parmesan cheese. Mince artichoke hearts in food processor and add to bowl.

STRAIN the sun-dried tomatoes and put in small bowl. Add garlic and olive oil and let tomatoes sit in this mixture for about 5 minutes. Strain tomatoes to remove excess olive oil and add to trout mixture. Mince red onion in food processor and add to trout mixture. Blend all ingredients well and chill for at least 1 hour.

WHEN ready to serve, heat oven to 400 degrees. Portion about 1 cup of dip into individual oven-safe ceramic dishes. Bake dishes in 400-degree oven for about 15 minutes. Once done, sprinkle with chives and Parmesan, and serve with toasted sourdough bread.

***Serves 10***

*Wine suggestion: Domaine de la Perriere Sancerre, Italy*

# Gazpacho

## Ingredients

- 15 *Roma tomatoes*
- 2 *cucumbers, peeled & seeded*
- 1 *red bell pepper, seeded*
- 2 *green bell peppers, seeded*
- ½ *yellow onion*
- 3 *celery stalks*
- 2 *limes, juiced*
- 2 *cups V-8 tomato juice*
- 1 *tablespoon olive oil*
- ½ *tablespoon garlic, minced*
- 1 *tablespoon cumin*
- 1 *tablespoon Tabasco*
- 2 *tablespoons salt*
- 2 *tablespoons black pepper*
- ¼ *cup red wine vinegar*
- 2 *tablespoons fresh basil, finely minced*
- *sour cream (optional)*
- *tortilla chips (optional)*

## Preparation

CHOP tomatoes, cucumbers, peppers, onion, and celery into medium size pieces, small enough to fit through the opening of a food processor. Mince all the pieces in a food processor and transfer to a bowl. Squeeze fresh lime juice into mixture. Add V-8 juice, olive oil, garlic, cumin, Tabasco, salt, pepper, and red wine vinegar to bowl. Add minced basil and mix all ingredients well. Chill for at least 2 hours.

WHEN ready to serve, ladle Gazpacho into soup cups and place a dollop of sour cream over the top, and serve with tortilla chips, if desired.

***Yield: approximately 1 gallon***

*Wine suggestion: Santa Cristina Pinot Grigio, Italy*

# Shrimp and Andouille Sausage Jambalaya

## Ingredients

*¼ cup olive oil*
*1¼ pounds Italian sausage*
*1 tablespoon garlic, minced*
*2 cups yellow onion, diced*
*2 cups celery, diced*
*2 cups red bell pepper, diced*
*1 tablespoon dry thyme*
*1 pounds Andouille Sausage*
*4 tablespoons Cajun seasoning*
*1 tablespoon dry parsley*
*½ tablespoon black pepper*
*½ cup flour*
*23 ounces V-8 juice*
*12 cups water*
*1½ tablespoons clam base*
*3 tablespoons chicken base*
*2½ pounds Black Tiger shrimp (41-60 count)*
*Cooked Rice (recipe follows)*
*fresh basil, chiffonade, for garnish*

## Preparation

IN A large soup kettle, heat olive oil, add Italian sausage, and cook until brown. Add garlic, onion, celery, and bell pepper, and cook until onion is tender. Add thyme, Andouille sausage, Cajun seasoning, parsley, and pepper, mixing in well. Add flour and cook, stirring constantly, for about 3 minutes. Then add V-8, water, clam and chicken bases, and shrimp. Let mixture simmer for 15 minutes.

PLACE about 1 cup Cooked Rice in the center of each soup bowl and ladle the jambalaya around rice. Garnish with the fresh basil.

***Serves 24***

*Wine suggestion: La Posta Malbec, Argentina*

## For the Cooked Rice

*8 cups rice*
*16 cups water*
*2 tablespoons butter*
*2 tablespoons salt*

BRING the water to a boil and add butter and salt. Add rice and bring back to a boil. Reduce heat to low, cover, and cook rice for about 15 minutes.

# Pan Seared Alaskan Sea Scallops

*with Jalapeño Cream Sauce*

## Ingredients

*12 20-ct. Alaskan sea scallops*
*Lawry's Seasoned Salt*
*¼ cup olive oil*
*Jalapeno Cream Sauce (recipe follows)*

## Preparation

SEASON scallops with Lawry's Seasoned Salt. Place ¼ cup olive oil in a sauté pan and heat until oil begins to smoke. Reduce heat to medium and place scallops in oil. Cook on each side until brown, about 3 minutes per side.

IN A saucepan, bring Jalapeno Cream Sauce to a simmer. Place scallops on plates and top with about ½ ounce of sauce on each scallop.

***Serves 4***

*Wine suggestions: Coppola Sauvignon Blanc or Merryvale "Staumont" Chardonnay, both from Napa*

## For the Jalapeño Cream Sauce

*3 large tomatoes*
*olive oil*
*3 jalapeño peppers, halved & seeded*
*1 yellow onion, julienned*
*8 garlic cloves*
*1 tablespoon salt*
*1 tablespoon black pepper*
*1 cup cilantro, minced*
*2 cups heavy cream*

HEAT broiler. Coat tomatoes with olive oil and place under hot broiler. Broil until skin is marked and starts to peel.

HEAT oven to 500 degrees. Sauté the jalapenos, onion, and garlic in olive oil until the onion starts to brown. Place the broiled tomatoes on top of onion mixture and place the sauté pan in the 500-degree oven for 15 minutes. Remove from oven and chill mixture for 1 hour in refrigerator.

PLACE the chilled ingredients in food processor along with the salt, pepper, and cilantro, and purée. Slowly mix in the heavy cream and set aside or refrigerate until ready to use.

***Yield: about 4 cups***

# Roasted Jamaican Jerk Chicken

The marinade in this recipe can be used for up to 4 batches, so long as it is refrigerated and used within 2 weeks.

## Ingredients

- *3 3-pound chickens*
- *8 cups orange juice*
- *4 cups soy sauce*
- *3 cups apple cider vinegar*
- *1 cup kosher salt*
- *1 cup sugar*
- *3 cups green onions, chopped*
- *1 cup jalapeno peppers, minced*
- *4 tablespoons ground black pepper*
- *4 ground dry sage*
- *3 tablespoons garlic, minced*
- *3 cups McCormick jerk seasoning*
- *1 cup fresh lime juice*
- *8 cups yellow onion, chopped*
- *½ gallon water*

## Preparation

COMBINE all the ingredients, except the chickens, in a bucket and mix well. Add the chickens and marinate in the refrigerator for at least 24 hours.

WHEN ready to cook, heat oven to 300 degrees. Remove chickens from marinade and lay them on a sheet pan, breast side down. Roast chickens in 300-degree oven for about 1-1/2 hours, or until internal temperature is 165°. When done, remove from oven and reserve pan drippings. Let chickens rest for 10 minutes and then cut them in half and pull out rib bones.

SERVE chickens with pan drippings drizzled over them.

***Serves 6 – 8***

*Wine suggestion: Valley of the Moon Pinot Blanc, Sonoma*

# Double Black Diamond Chocolate Ganache

This is the signature dessert of the Roosevelt Tavern.

## Ingredients

- *6 ounces clarified butter*
- *2 cups graham cracker crumbs*
- *1 ounce Kahlua coffee liquor*
- *2 ounces powdered sugar*
- *2 cups heavy whipping cream*
- *16 ounces semisweet dark chocolate, shaved*
- *8 ounces white chocolate*

## Preparation

MELT butter and add graham cracker crumbs, mixing well to combine. Place mix in an 11-inch pie pan, one that has ripples on the sides. Form crust on bottom of pan, pushing crust to the sides. Leaves sides slightly thicker than base.

BRING some water to boil in a saucepot, and place a large stainless steel bowl over the pot, to make a bain marie. Put coffee liquor, powdered sugar, and heavy cream into the bowl. Mix well until all the sugar is dissolved. Mix in the dark chocolate with a whisk until there are no more lumps. Pour chocolate mix into the crust in the pie pan. Spread evenly to the edges.

USING the same boiling water but a different bowl, melt the white chocolate until it is smooth. With the white chocolate, make 4 concentric circles on the pie. This is easier if you put the melted white chocolate in a squeeze bottle. Using a toothpick, start in the center of the pie and run a line through the 4 white circles to the outer edge of the pie. Then, about ½ inch from that line, run the toothpick in the reverse direction, starting at the edge and going toward the center. Continue running alternate lines until the whole pie is done. The finished product should resemble a flower design.

LET the pie cool for 4 hours in the refrigerator. When ready to serve, cut the pie on every fourth ripple and you should get 16 slices.

***Serves 16***

# *The Sawtooth Club*

231 Main Street
Ketchum, ID 83340
208-726-5233

Grill with bar menu open 5:00pm to 11:00pm
Dining Room open 5:30pm to 10:00pm

# The Sawtooth Club

### Tom Nickel, Owner

The Sawtooth Club has a long and interesting history in Sun Valley. In the early 1930s Idaho allowed gambling if the community approved it. Ketchum was one of the towns that took advantage of this sport. The Union Pacific Railroad owned the luxurious Sun Valley Resort, and did not allow gambling on resort property. Consequently many of the guests of the resort, including movie stars and European royalty, made the one-mile trek into Ketchum to gamble at poker, roulette, dice, and other games. The Sawtooth Club was a popular gambling spot during this era until table gaming was outlawed in Idaho in 1949.

The popularity of The Sawtooth Club continued, however. One of its most famous regular patrons was Papa Hemingway. As Hunter S. Thompson wrote in his book *The Great Shark Hunt*, "He could sit in the Sawtooth Club and talk with men who felt the same way de did about life, even if they were not so articulate. In this congenial atmosphere he felt he could get away from the pressures of a world gone mad and 'write truly' about life as he had in the past".

Today The Sawtooth Club sports a new wood-sided exterior in keeping with downtown Ketchum, but the local camaraderie remains the same. The original first floor houses a classic western bar and serves lighter fare in front of the cozy fireplace. For more formal dining, climb the stairs to the rustic yet elegant dining room. In the summer, guests can also enjoy their meals on the canopied terrace deck overlooking Main Street. Though the hours state that the restaurant closes at 10:00pm, guests are never pushed out the door, but allowed to linger over their meals, as befits true western hospitality.

The food is exceptional, ranging from Pacific Rim influences to luscious steaks, chops, and seafood cooked over a fire with mesquite wood imported from Texas. The wood-grilled duck is a specialty of the house, and the vegetables served with dinner are also grilled on the mesquite fire, usually just brushed with olive oil and balsamic vinegar to let their fresh flavors shine through. A full bar and an exceptional wine list compliment the elegantly prepared meals, and the excellent service by the wait staff adds the perfect touch. Any trip to Ketchum is not complete without a dinner or a libation and hors d'oeuvres at The Sawtooth Club.

# House-smoked Salmon and Artichoke Dip

The main thing I like about this dish is that we smoke our own fresh fish daily, using a special brine.

## Ingredients

*44 ounces canned artichoke hearts*
*2 cups sun-dried tomatoes*
*2 cups red onion*
*1 pound smoked salmon*
*1 5-pound block cream cheese*
*4 cups Parmesan cheese, shredded*
*4 cups mayonnaise*
*shredded Parmesan, for garnish*
*chopped green onions, for garnish*
*crustini or garlic bread*

## Preparation

PURÉE the artichoke hearts in a robo coup or food processor with the sun-dried tomatoes, onion, salmon, and cream cheese. Mix in the Parmesan and mayonnaise. Keep chilled in refrigerator until ready to serve.

TO SERVE, heat oven to 425 degrees. Fill small ceramic soup cups to about 2/3 with the dip. Sprinkle Parmesan cheese over the top and bake in the oven for about 10 to 12 minutes, until the cheese is golden brown. Garnish with chopped green onions and serve with crustini or garlic bread.

***Yield: 4 quarts***

*Wine suggestion: Adelsheim Pinot Gris, Oregon*

# Chicken Senegalese

This is a dish that the owner, Tom Nickel, got from a trip to Africa in 1986. The original recipe was actually a soup. Through trial and error he and his head chef came up with this wonderful dish for chicken. This is something everyone will enjoy and is easy to make. Serve with wild rice.

## Ingredients

- 4 *5-ounce chicken breasts*
- ½ *cup flour*
- ¼ *cup clarified butter*
- ½ *teaspoon shallot, chopped fine*
- ¼ *cup sherry*
- ¼ *cup apple juice*
- 1 *teaspoon Madras style curry powder*
- ½ *cup heavy cream*
- ¼ *Granny Smith apple, sliced for garnish*
- *paprika for garnish*

## Preparation

PLACE chicken breasts on clean cutting board and cut off excess fat, plus membrane. Toss chicken breasts in flour. Pour clarified butter into a sauté pan; just enough to coat the bottom of the pan. Wait until the pan is hot and sear both sides of the chicken breasts. Add chopped shallot and sauté for 1-2 minutes. Add sherry, apple juice, and curry, and simmer to reduce by half. Add heavy cream and reduce by half. Sauce will thicken as it cooks.

PLACE 2 chicken breasts on each plate and top with the apple slices. Pour the sauce over the apple slices and garnish with paprika.

***Serves 2***

*Wine suggestion: Von Hoevel Estate Dry Riesling, Germany*

# Rack of Lamb

I have suggested a nice Pinot Noir from Phantom Hill in Oregon. The owner of the vineyard and the winemaker lives in Ketchum.

## Ingredients

*4-6 8-ounce racks of lamb*
*4 cups olive oil*
*2 cups soy sauce*
*1 cup red wine*
*1 cup sherry*
*4 tablespoons rosemary*
*4 tablespoons thyme*
*4 tablespoons garlic, chopped*
*2 bunches green onions, chopped*

## Preparation

COMBINE all the ingredients except the lamb. Place lamb racks in the marinade for 2 to 6 hours.

HEAT oven to 475 degrees. Remove lamb from the marinade and place in large roasting pan. Roast in oven for 8 to 12 minutes, depending on desired degree of doneness.

MAKE a slice down the middle of each bone, and arrange on plate with your favorite starch and vegetable.

***Serves 4 – 6***

*Wine suggestion: Phantom Hill Pinot Noir, Willamette Valley, Oregon*

# Berry Crisps

## Ingredients

- *4 cups oatmeal*
- *2 teaspoons cinnamon*
- *1 cup flour*
- *1½ cups brown sugar*
- *1 pound chilled butter, cut into cubes*
- *5 pounds frozen berries, a mixture of blueberries, strawberries, blackberries & raspberries*
- *1 cup sugar*
- *½ cup cornstarch*
- *zest of 2 lemons*

## Preparation

HEAT oven to 375 degrees. Mix oatmeal, cinnamon, flour, brown sugar, and butter cubes together in a mixing bowl with a paddle. Mix well. Be sure to cover mixing bowl with a towel because you will create a small mess. Set aside.

PLACE frozen berries on a sheet pan or cookie sheet and place in the oven until thawed. Place the sugar, cornstarch, and lemon zest in a mixing bowl and add the thawed berries while still warm, so that the cornstarch has time to activate. Stir gently to combine.

PLACE 4 ounces of the berry mixture into individual ovenproof dishes, and top with the oatmeal topping, covering berries completely. Bake in the 375-degree oven for 18 minutes.

SERVE warm with your favorite ice cream.

***Serves 13***

320 S. Main Street
Hailey, ID 83333
208-788-1223

Dinner daily 5:00pm to 10:00pm

# CK's

### *Chris Kastner, Owner/Chef*
### *Rebecca Kastner, Owner*

Down the road from the popular Sun Valley Ski Resort is the lovely little town of Hailey, founded in 1880 by John Hailey. With the mining boom in the valley during the late 19th century, Hailey boasted eighteen saloons and twelve gambling parlors, as well as three daily newspapers. It is also the birthplace of Ezra Pound, the infamous 20th century poet. Today, Hailey is a much quieter town of about 6,000, with a thriving art scene and some very fine dining.

On the corner of Pine and Main Streets sits a small house that has undergone a beautiful transformation into a bastion of the Slow-Food Movement. CK's is the result of a vision of Chris Kastner and his business partner and wife, Rebecca. Chris has been in the restaurant business for 30 years, starting as a dishwasher at the Sun Valley Inn. After working in many of the Sun Valley area restaurants, Chris and Rebecca decided to do their own thing and open CK's. Their emphasis is on the use of local organic produce that is in season. With a strong environmental ethic, the Kastner's like to feature produce and meats that are grown and raised in an environmentally friendly manner. The culinary emphasis is on regional Northwest cuisine, with inspiration drawn from the cuisines of Europe, the Middle East, Asia, and the Americas, and in keeping with the true nature of these areas. The restaurant also features dishes created in the slow-food style, dishes that are allowed to cook slowly to bring out all the different flavors of the fresh ingredients. A very nice wine list specializes in the wines of the Northwest, along with an ample selection of microbrews.

The restaurant is truly a family affair, with Chris serving as chef and main creator of the succulent dishes, and Rebecca developing a luscious dessert menu as well as managing the wine list and the front of the house. Their two children, Simone and Gavin, are also a vital part of the operation. Simone makes all the ice creams and sorbets as well as working the line some nights, and Gavin works in the kitchen and also the dining room.

The house has been painstakingly remodeled to create an intimate dining experience with tables set apart for privacy, and a lovely outdoor patio for summer dining. Your dining experience will be a delight with the comfortable surroundings and the personalized care that you will receive from the experienced wait staff.

# Cherry Soup

This is on our menu as long as the Emmett cherry season lasts. Kurtis from Waterwheel Gardens brings us the best cherries, peaches, and berries. Other fruits can be used for this soup when they are at their peak. Peaches make a great soup with a few blackberries thrown in.

## Ingredients

- *1 tablespoon fresh ginger, grated*
- *1 star anise pod*
- *1 1-inch cinnamon stick*
- *1 Serrano chili, seeded and sliced*
- *1 lemon, zested and juiced*
- *1 orange, zested and juiced*
- *2 cups gewürztraminer, moscato, or Riesling*
- *6 cups good water*
- *½ cup sugar*
- *1 vanilla bean, split*
- *4 quarts cherries, pitted*
- *1 tablespoon lemon juice*
- *1 tablespoon balsamic vinegar*
- *salt to taste*
- *whipped plain yogurt for garnish*

## Preparation

IN A non-reactive pot, combine ginger, anise, cinnamon, chili, lemon, orange, wine, water, sugar, and vanilla bean. Simmer for 20 minutes and strain. Return 3 cups of this stock to the pot and add the cherries. Reserve the remaining stock to adjust thickness.

BRING the mixture to a simmer and continue simmering for 20 minutes. Purée and then strain through a food mill. Adjust thickness with some of the remaining stock, and adjust acidity with the lemon juice and balsamic vinegar. Salt to taste. Chill. When ready to serve, ladle into individual bowls and drizzle whipped yogurt on.

***Yield: about 3 quarts***

*Wine suggestion: Buty's Semillon/Sauvignon Blance*

# Grilled Idaho Trout

*with Red Curry Corn and Carolina Dirty Tartar Sauce*

One of our signature dishes is the grilled trout. The trout are raised 75 miles away at Canyon Trout Farm. In the summer, all the vegetables are grown locally. CK's BBQ Spice is great on all things grilled, and can be used as a blackening spice too.

## Ingredients

- *4 10-ounce boneless Idaho trout filets*
- *CK's BBQ Spice to taste (recipe follows)*
- *olive oil*
- *Red Curry Corn (recipe follows)*
- *Carolina Dirty Tartar Sauce (recipe follows)*

## Preparation

RUB trout filets generously with CK's BBQ Spice and brush with olive oil. Set aside until ready to grill.

WHILE corn is cooking, spray grill surface with vegetable oil and heat grill. Grill trout on hot grill, inside of trout down first, for about 3 minutes. Flip, and grill on skin side for another 3 minutes. Serve with the Red Curry Corn and Carolina Dirty Tartar Sauce.

***Serves 4***

*Wine suggestion: Cakebread Sauvignon Blanc*

## For the CK's BBQ Spice

- *½ cup chili powder*
- *2 tablespoons whole dried basil leaves*
- *2 tablespoons whole dried thyme leaves*
- *2 tablespoons whole dried oregano leaves*
- *3 tablespoons fresh ground black pepper*
- *1 cup Old Bay seasoning*
- *1 tablespoon Colman's dried mustard powder*

MIX all ingredients together and store in an airtight container.

## For the Carolina Dirty Tartar Sauce

- *2 cups mayonnaise*
- *2 tablespoons Creole mustard*
- *1 teaspoon CK's BBQ Spice*
- *½ teaspoon black pepper*
- *½ cup green onion, sliced thin*
- *⅓ cup Italian parsley, chopped*
- *1 teaspoon Worcestershire sauce*
- *4 medium dill pickles, diced*
- *2 tablespoons capers, rinsed, drained, & coarsely chopped*
- *1 teaspoon Tabasco*
- *¼ cup lemon juice*
- *salt to taste*

COMBINE in a big bowl, adjusting salt and acid with lemon juice. This will keep in refrigerator for two weeks.

## For the Red Curry Corn

- 6 *ears corn, decobbed (about 3 cups)*
- 1 *tablespoon olive oil*
- 1 *medium onion, ¼-inch dice*
- 1 *jalapeno, seeded and minced*
- 1 *tablespoon garlic, minced*
- 1 *kaffir lime leaf, thinly sliced*
- 1 *teaspoon whole dark mustard seeds*
- 1 *teaspoon red curry paste*
- ¾ *cup stock or water*
- ¾ *cup coconut milk*
- 1 *tablespoon lime juice*
- *salt to taste*

HEAT a 2-quart saucepan with the olive oil and add onion, jalapeno, garlic, kaffir leaf, mustard seeds, and curry paste. Sauté for 1 to 2 minutes just to soften, not brown. Add the corn, stir in the liquids, bring to a simmer and cook 5 minutes, just until the liquid reduces and develops some body. Adjust seasoning.

*Cowboys and saddle ponies in camp on the range.*

# Gaucho Steak

*with Chimi Churi and Roasted Cauliflower with Caramelized Shallots*

This traditional Argentine dish has become a CK's favorite. We use a shoulder tenderloin steak, but rib eye, New York, or sirloin also work well, as does lamb and chicken.

## Ingredients

- *4 10-ounce shoulder tenderloin steaks*
- *1 cup warm water*
- *2 tablespoons kosher salt*
- *1 teaspoon cayenne pepper*
- *Chimi Churri Sauce (recipe follows)*
- *Roasted Cauliflower with Caramelized Shallots (recipe follows)*

## Preparation

HEAT grill. Combine water, salt, and pepper. Baste twice on meat while grilling. This salts and seasons the meat, but be careful not to overdo it or it will be too salty. Grill to desired temperature.

TO SERVE, place a steak on each plate along with a generous helping of Roasted Cauliflower. With a spoon or small ladle, place some of the Chimi Churri Sauce around the plate and over the cauliflower. Place more Chimi Churri Sauce in a serving bowl for those who wish more.

***Serves 4***

*Wine suggestion: a big, hearty Syrah, like Basal from Walla Walla, Washington*

## For the Chimi Churri Sauce

- *2 cups Italian parsley, rough chop*
- *¼ cup fresh oregano, rough chop*
- *2 tablespoons garlic, minced*
- *2 tablespoons shallots, sliced*
- *1 teaspoon red pepper flakes, crushed*
- *1½ teaspoons salt*
- *1½ teaspoons black pepper*
- *2 tablespoons lemon juice*
- *2 tablespoons sherry vinegar*
- *1¼ cups olive oil*

IN A food processor combine all the herbs and spices. Pulse 4 or 5 times, add the lemon juice and vinegar and blend for 5 seconds. While processor is on, pour in olive oil over a count of 5, and then turn off. You are trying to achieve an herb-olive oil sauce, not too runny and definitely not too pasty. Adjust as needed with olive oil and/or a little water.

This recipe makes more than you will need, but is good on anything and keeps well in the refrigerator. The color will fade over time, though.

### For the Roasted Cauliflower with Caramelized Onions

- 1 *head cauliflower, broken into bite-size pieces*
- 2 *tablespoons olive oil*
- 1 *tablespoon butter*
- ½ *cup shallots, julienne*
- ¼ *cup parsley, chopped*
- *salt and black pepper to taste*

HEAT oven to 400 degrees. Heat a wide heavy skillet with olive oil and butter. Add shallots and toss to coat. Add cauliflower, toss, and season with salt and pepper. Place in 400-degree oven for 15 minutes. Stir halfway through. Add the parsley just before serving.

*Gaucho Steak*

# Lamb Ragu

*with Eggplant, Fingerling Potatoes, and Pecorino Cheese*

Our lamb is raised 60 miles away in the mountains and high desert at Lava Lake Ranch. The folks at Lava Lake are very unique in the ranching world of Idaho. They are aggressively undertaking rehabilitating their grazing lands, and restoring habitat for the wild animals that live there as well. They are known as "wolf lovers" by their skeptical ranching neighbors for their strong belief that they can ranch and co-exist with the wolves and coyotes. They oversee the processing of their animals as well. The animals spend no time on a feedlot and have the natural hormone-free grass-fed flavor that makes their lamb so special and delicious. This dish is also representative of our nightly Slo-Food menu items. They are traditional ethnic fare from around the world, usually long-cooking stew and braised meat dishes; not always lamb, sometimes beef, pork, or chicken. Our clientele love these homey dishes.

## Ingredients

- *2 pounds lamb shoulder stew meat, 1- to 2-inch dice*
- *1 large yellow onion, ½-inch dice*
- *6 garlic cloves, smashed & rough chopped*
- *2 bay leaves*
- *6 sprigs fresh rosemary, rough chopped*
- *½ cup olive oil*
- *black pepper to taste*
- *3 cups red wine*
- *3 cups chicken stock*
- *1 large eggplant, peeled 1-inch dice*
- *1 pound fingerling potatoes, pre-cooked & kept warm*
- *1 cup good quality pecorino cheese, grated*

## Preparation

COMBINE the lamb, onion, garlic, herbs, olive oil, and pepper in a bowl and marinate overnight.

THE next day, heat oven to 450 degrees. Put the lamb and its marinade in a Dutch oven or brazier large enough to hold it and the liquids, which will be added later. Roast the lamb, uncovered, for about 40 minutes, or until it is well browned. Stir a few times during this process.

REMOVE the brazier and reduce the oven temperature to 325 degrees. Add the wine and stock to the brazier and bring to a simmer on the stove. Cover, and put back in 325-degree oven to bake for about 2 hours, or just about fork tender.

SAUTÉ the eggplant in olive oil and reserve. When meat is just fork tender, remove to stove and bring oven temperature up to 400 degrees. Add sautéed eggplant and cooked potatoes to the ragu, stirring to combine. Bring to a simmer; sprinkle the top with cheese, and place back in oven, uncovered for 20 minutes, just until the cheese begins to brown and gratinée nicely.

THE cheese will help the sauce thicken and give it body. You could do this process up to 3 days ahead, and then reheat and add the cheese when ready to serve.

***Serves 6***

*Wine suggestion: great with a good Italian wine like Avignonesi Vino Nobile di Montepulciano 2001*

## Fresh Lime Pie

*with Meyers Whipped Cream*

### Ingredients

- 2 *packages graham crackers*
- 10 *ounces butter, melted*
- 6 *tablespoons granulated sugar*
- 1 *cup egg yolks*
- 3 *tablespoons lime zest*
- 1½ *cups fresh lime juice*
- 3 *cans sweetened condensed milk*
- 1 *cup whipping cream*
- 2 *tablespoons powdered sugar*
- 1 *tablespoon Meyers rum*

### Preparation

HEAT oven to 350 degrees. Grind graham crackers in food processor, adding granulated sugar and butter. Gently but firmly press mixture into 2 pie pans to form crusts. Bake in 350-degree oven for 15 minutes. Cool before filling.

MIX egg yolks and lime zest for 3 minutes in mixer. Add lime juice and evaporated milk and mix well. Let mixture sit for a few minutes to thicken up. Pour into pie shells and bake at 350 degrees for 20 minutes, or until set. Cool, and then chill in refrigerator until service.

JUST before serving, whip cream, powdered sugar and rum in mixer. Serve on top of pie.

***Yield: 2 pies***

*Shepherds and wagon at the Edward Trafton place near Oasis in Teton County (then Fremont County), June, 1905. Photo by A. W. Stevens.*

# The Continental Bistro

140 South Main Street
Old Town
Pocatello, ID 83204
208-233-4433

Serving Monday thru Saturday
Lunch 11:00am to 5:00pm
Dinner 5:00pm to 10:00pm

# The Continental Bistro

*John B Perryman, Rob Wiscombe, Bob Pehrsson, Dale Pehrsson, Owners*

Pocatello, Idaho is known as the Gate City to the Northwest, and The Continental Bistro is one of its premier restaurants. The Continental Bistro and the Bistro Pub occupy a unique place in the historic Old Town district of the city. Established in 1993, the bistro offers fine dining in a casual bistro setting. The pub, with an Irish Georgian pub theme serves premium spirits, Northwest micro brews, and an extensive award-winning wine list, having won the prestigious *Award of Excellence* by the *Wine Spectator* magazine.

The pub resides within the Benedicte Wrensted property of 1908-1912. Ms. Wrensted was made famous by her photographs of the indigenous Native Americans and the local area which are on display at The Smithsonian Institute in Washington, D.C. The lovely enclosed open-air garden allows seasonal dining, and spans the famous Princess Theatre brick wall of the turn of the last century. The Princess Theatre gained notoriety in the 1954 film "A Star Is Born", starring Judy Garland. In the film, she sings the hit song, "I was born in a trunk at the Princess Theatre in Pocatello, Idaho". The garden features Belgian cobblestone and Italian slate with wrought iron tables and chairs. Floral pots and a fountain complete the scene reminiscent of a European café. In the summer the garden plays host to the Annual Summer Garden Music Festival where local artists play into the summer night. The festival is held every Wednesday in the summer, with entertainment beginning at 7:30pm, weather permitting. The bistro itself is housed in the former Kane Grocery and Fords Pool Hall property where Jack Dempsey was noted as having a prizefight while working in the Gate City. The original brick wall is exposed to lend a rustic and casual ambience to the dining experience.

The bistro's cuisine combines contemporary American fare with culinary influences from France, Italy, and Germany. For starters, try a cup of the fabulous Crawfish Bisque, sure to get your taste buds ready for more. Along with great American steaks, you will find a German Jägerschnitzel, a veal scaloppini served with a Jäger cream sauce over spätzle, and an Italian Chicken and Artichoke Mostaccioli, composed of roasted chicken, artichoke hearts and Roma tomatoes in a basil carbonara sauce tossed with quill-shaped pasta. The Italian Cioppino is a succulent seafood stew combining crab claws, shrimp, clams, ahi tuna in a spicy tomato broth. With all this variety, you can be assured that everyone in your party will find a special pasta or entrée and a special beverage to pair perfectly.

# Peel and Eat Garlic Shrimp

This reception favorite is the hallmark of any get together.

## Ingredients

*2 pounds medium shrimp, shell on*
*½ pound margarine*
*3 scallions, chopped*
*2 tablespoons garlic, chopped*
*1 tablespoon black pepper, cracked*
*1 lemon, cut into wedges*
*⅓ cup white wine*
*2 tablespoons cornstarch, mixed with 2 tablespoons of water*
*hot sauce or Cajun seasoning to taste*
*salt to taste*

## Preparation

SAUTÉ the first five ingredients on high heat until shrimp are cooked through. This will take about five minutes. Squeeze the lemon into the pan, adding the wedges to the pan as well. Add the wine and heat to just below boiling. Mix in the cornstarch mixture, heating until thick to create a tasty sauce. Add seasonings to taste. These shrimp can be eaten hot or cold.

IF SERVED hot, the shrimp are ready and could now be served on a bed of shredded lettuce with additional lemon. If served cold, use the following "ice-bath" method. To cool quickly, place shrimp in a bowl into which they fit easily. Place this bowl inside another bowl that has at least two trays of ice and ample cold water in it. Allow shrimp to stand for several minutes; stir, and repeat. The shrimp should be chilled in about 30 minutes.

***Serves 4–8***

*Beverage suggestions: New Belgium Brewing Co., Loft Ale or Merryvale "Starmont" Chardonnay, Napa Valley*

# Parmesan Crusted Salmon Salad

Parmesan cheese and salmon are not often paired together, but in this recipe it works. Broiling the salmon with the Parmesan on top keeps the fish moist, while creating a tasty, crispy crust. Enjoy this longstanding Bistro favorite for lunch or dinner.

## Ingredients

*2 ounces orange juice concentrate, thawed*
*splash of rice wine vinegar, to taste*
*1 tablespoon honey*
*2 tablespoons olive oil*
*2 4-ounce salmon filets*
*salt and pepper*
*¼ cup fresh Parmesan cheese, grated*
*salad greens*
*1 tomato, wedged*
*1 red onion, sliced*

## Preparation

TO MAKE dressing, stir the orange juice concentrate and rice wine vinegar together in a mixing bowl. Add the honey, and then slowly incorporate the olive oil. Place aside until plating the dish.

PREHEAT broiler. Season the filets with salt and pepper and place them on a broiler pan. Top with the Parmesan cheese and place under broiler for 3-5 minutes, until salmon begins to flake to the touch. Be careful not to burn the cheese. If this begins to happen, change oven setting to bake and cook until done.

TO BEGIN the plating process, pour the dressing over your favorite variety of greens. Serve the warm salmon filets over the greens along with any leftover dressing on the side. Garnish the plate with sliced onion and tomato.

***Serves 2***

*Wine Suggestions: La Crema Pinot Noir or Corton-Charlemagne Grand Cru Bonneau du Martray White Burgundy.*

# Garlic Shrimp and Pappardelle Pasta

For those who like seafood in a tomato sauce with pasta this is a must try! Garlic is important in the cooking that we do, but at the restaurant, we must, of course, exercise moderation. At home, however, you can go for the gusto!

## Ingredients

*½ pound medium shrimp, peeled & deveined*
*2 teaspoons garlic, chopped*
*¼ cup button mushrooms, sliced*
*2 cups prepared pasta sauce*
*3 sprigs fresh basil, chopped*
*¼ cup spinach, chopped*
*1 Roma tomato, chopped*
*½ cup chicken broth*
*salt and pepper to taste*
*12 ounces lasagna noodles, cooked*
*Parmesan cheese, grated*

## Preparation

IN A hot skillet or sauté pan, add the olive oil, garlic, mushrooms, and shrimp. Cook for about 4 minutes at medium high heat. Add the pasta sauce to the mixture, bringing it to a slow simmer. Add the basil, spinach, tomatoes, and the chicken broth, cooking for about 3 more minutes. Season with salt and pepper to taste. Serve over cooked lasagna noodles that are cut into strips. Top with grated Parmesan cheese.

***Serves 2-4***

*Wine Suggestions: Frescobaldi-Robert Mondavi Lucente, Tuscany or Luna di Luna Chardonnay-Pinot Grigio*

# Triple Layered Cappuccino and Brownie Mousse

## Ingredients

- ⅓ *cup hot water*
- 2 *teaspoons instant espresso granules, divided*
- ½ *box brownie mix (2 cups)*
- 2 *teaspoons vanilla extract, divided*
- *non-stick cooking spray*
- ¾ *cup milk*
- 3 *tablespoons Frangelico or other nut flavored liqueur, divided*
- 1 *package chocolate flavored instant pudding mix*
- 3 *cups whipped topping, thawed & divided*
- *espresso beans or hazelnuts, chopped (optional)*

## Preparation

HEAT the oven to 350 degrees. Combine hot water and 1 teaspoon espresso granules in a medium bowl and mix. Add the brownie mix and 1 teaspoon of the vanilla; mix until well blended. Pour the mixture into a 9-inch pie plate that has been well coated with cooking spray. Bake at 350 degrees for about 20 minutes, or until a knife inserted into the brownie comes out almost clean. Let the brownie cool completely.

COMBINE the milk, 2 tablespoons Frangelico, 1 teaspoon vanilla, and pudding mix. Blend this with a mixer on low for 30 seconds, then on medium speed for 30 more seconds. Gently fold in 1½ cups whipped topping. Spread the pudding mixture evenly over the brownie.

IN A bowl, mix the remaining 1 teaspoon of espresso granules and Frangelico. Gently fold in the remaining 1½ cups of whipped topping. Spread whipped topping over the pudding mixture. If you wish, garnish with either espresso beans or hazelnuts, plain or chocolate covered. Serve immediately, or if you are serving later, loosely cover and store in refrigerator.

***Serves 1–6***

*Beverage suggestions: Pedro Domecq, Amontillado, Sherry or Graham's 10-year Tawny Port or Seattle's Best, organic, fair trade, shade-grown, French roast coffee.*

# Remo's

160 West Cedar
Pocatello, ID 83201
208-233-1710

Monday - Thursday
11:30am to 9:00pm
Friday - Saturday
11:30am to 10:00pm
Closed Sunday

# Remo's

### *Bob "Hornet" Thronson, Owner*

Get ready to enjoy some classic Italian culinary treats when you step into the warm and comfortable atmosphere of Remo's in Pocatello. Although the restaurant can accommodate a large number of guests, the arrangement of several small rooms that flow into each other gives the diner a more intimate feeling. Brick half walls and stucco interlaced with dark timbers add to the ambiance, as does the large fireplace in the front room. In summer, up to 80 guests can be accommodated on the vine-covered patio at the front of the restaurant.

Remo's began its life in 1956 as Gil's Pizzeria, owned by Gilbert and Mary Paolino. The Grayson and Colaianni families purchased the restaurant from the Paolino's in 1962, did extensive remodeling and renamed it Remo's. In 1973, Jim Grayson took over the Colaianni family's interest and completely renovated the restaurant, doubling its seating capacity. In October 1986 Hornet Thronson bought ownership from Jim and Virgie Grayson. He added the outside patio the following year and added a private dining room in 1991.

In 1987 Remo's started an ambitious journey, with a goal to develop a world-class wine program for the restaurant. This was achieved by purchasing wine 'futures' on the best wines from the best vintages. The 'futures' were laid down in the wine cellar to continue aging. This ongoing long-term acquisition policy became a cornerstone of the development of Remo's wine program. After five years, some of the first of the 'futures' were placed on the wine list. This resulted in Remo's receiving the *Award of Excellence* from *Wine Spectator* in 1992. The restaurant won the award again in 1993 and, in 1994, was awarded the *Best of Award of Excellence* by the magazine. Remo's was one of only 365 restaurants in the world to be recognized by this award in 1994. The restaurant continued to win the Award of Excellence from 1995 to 2002. Today, the 24-page wine list is a delight to read, with a wide variety of wines from which to choose. This list contains many California wines, along with regional wines from Idaho, Oregon, and Washington, as well as selections from Italy, France, and Australia. There are close to 20 wines that are also served by the glass.

A relatively new addition to Remo's is the sushi menu that is served on Wednesday evenings from 5:00pm to 9:00pm, offering Pocatello a totally different concept from its classic Italian menu.

# Salmon Pâté

This is a great appetizer to make when you have excess salmon left from a dinner.

## Ingredients

- 1 *pound cooked salmon*
- ¼ *cup Maui or other sweet onion, finely diced*
- 1 *tablespoon fresh lemon juice*
- ¼ *tablespoon liquid smoke*
- 2 *tablespoons prepared horseradish*
- ½ *pound cream cheese*
- ½ *tablespoon salt*
- ½ *tablespoon white pepper*
- *crackers of your choice*

## Preparation

IN A mixer, thoroughly combine all ingredients. Mold the pâté on the center of a serving platter and spread the crackers around it. We prefer to use a butter cracker.

***Yield: about 3 cups***

# Chicken Puttanesca

The puttanesca sauce with this recipe keeps well, but it does get spicier with age.

## Ingredients

- *4 8-ounce chicken breasts*
- *5 cloves garlic, minced*
- *1 tablespoon capers*
- *1 teaspoon crushed red pepper*
- *1 tablespoon anchovy paste*
- *1 tablespoon olive oil*
- *½ cup hot water*
- *1 tablespoon chicken base*
- *1 small can tomato sauce*
- *1 tablespoon fresh parsley, chopped*
- *1 cup artichoke hearts*
- *½ cup black olives, sliced*
- *shredded Asiago cheese*

## Preparation

SAUTÉ garlic, capers, red peppers, and anchovy paste in olive oil. Dissolve the chicken base in the hot water and add to the sauté pan along with the tomato sauce. Bring the mixture to a boil and add the parsley, artichoke hearts, and olives. Keep warm.

HEAT broiler, and broil chicken breasts until they reach desired temperature.

TO SERVE, place chicken breasts on a platter or individual serving plates, pour sauce over chicken, and sprinkle shredded Asiago cheese over top. Enjoy!

***Serves 4***

# BBQ Flank or Skirt Steak

The key to this recipe is to sear the flavor into the meat by slightly charring the steak. The next key is the technique used to cut the steak. You will also be marinating the steak overnight, so plan ahead. This also makes a great hors d'oeuvre as well.

## Ingredients

*2 pounds flank or skirt steak*
*1-2 cups of your favorite BBQ marinade*
*½ cup oil or melted butter*

## Preparation

THE day before serving, trim any excess fat or silver skin off the steak. Place the steak in a shallow non-metallic pan, and marinate the meat in the BBQ sauce overnight.

ON THE day of service, preheat your grill. Remove steak from marinade and pat dry. Pour the butter or oil over the steak to coat. Lay steak on grill. Be very careful, as the oil will cause the fire to flame up. This flare is what you want in order to slightly char the steak. Move the steak around and turn over to char and sear in the flavors. Cook the steak to desired temperature and remove from grill.

WHEN cutting the steak, hold your knife at two 45-degree angles to the meat, against the grain. If the grain runs down the meat, turn your knife to a 45-degree angle to it and then turn it sideways to a 45-degree angle and cut through the meat this way. It will take out the toughness of the flank or skirt.

***Serves 4***

# About the Publishers

Chuck and Blanche started Wilderness Adventures Press, Inc. in 1993, publishing outdoor and sporting books. Along with hunting and fishing, they love fine dining, good wines, and traveling. They have always been able to "sniff out" the most outstanding and interesting restaurants in any city they visit.

On weekends, they experiment in the kitchen, cooking a variety of fish and meats, as well as preparing the harvest from their time in the field. This love of cooking has resulted in a large library of cookbooks, and has inspired them to create a series of cookbooks based on their love of travel and fine dining.

Chuck and Blanche make their home in Gallatin Gateway, Montana, along with their four German wirehaired pointers.

# Photo Copyrights/Credits

**Front Cover, left to right**: ©The Lodge at Hidden Lakes; © Mortimer's; ©Mortimer's; ©Blanche T. Johnson; ©Blanche T. Johnson; ©Appaloosa Museum and Heritage Center; ©CK's; ©Blanche T. Johnson; ©Emilio's; ©Idaho State Historical Society #74-193.31; © Chandlers. **Back Cover, left to right**: ©Mortimer's; ©Sand Creek Grill; ©Blanche T. Johnson; © Blanche T. Johnson; ©Chandler's; ©Andrae's.

**All interior photos**: ©Blanche T. Johnson or as noted below.

**i**: #538, ©Idaho State Historical Society; **vii**: (big) #60-99.56, (small) #75-190.10, ©Idaho State Historical Society; **xii(top)**: #74-193.31, ©Idaho State Historical Society; **xii**: © Appaloosa Museum and Heritage Center; **2**: ©Ivano's; **6**: #72-201.118, ©Idaho State Historical Society; **14, 15, 19**: ©Sand Creek Grill; **37, 42**: #76-165.4, #79-7.7, ©Idaho State Historical Society; **44**: ©The Wine Cellar; **48**: #76-165.15, ©Idaho State Historical Society; **55, 56, 59, 61**: ©Epicurean; **67, 68, 69, 70, 74**: ©Andrae's; **86**: #77-139.7, ©Idaho State Historical Society; **99, 103**: ©Cottonwood Grill; **105, 106, 109, 113**: ©Emilio's; **114**: ©Appaloosa Museum and Heritage Center; **115, 116(bottom), 118**: ©The Gamekeeper Restaurant; **122**: ©Le Café de Paris; **135, 136**: ©Mortimer's; **141, 142, 147**: ©Chandler's; **150**: ©Andrew Kent; **156**: #72-103.4, ©Idaho State Historical Society; **181, 182, 187**: ©CK's; **185**: ©Appaloosa Museum and Heritage Center; **190**: #P1985-42-33/G, ©Idaho State Historical Society; **192, 195**: ©The Continental Bistro.

# Culinary Sources

This list is provided for your convenience. While many of the suggested suppliers have been recommended, not all suppliers have been individually checked out. We do not endorse any particular vendor or supplier.

**Broken Arrow Ranch**
Antelope, venison, wild boar, sausages
Ingram, TX
800-962-4263
www.brokenarrowranch.com

**Caviar Direct**
Foreign & domestic caviar
800-650-2828
www.caviar-direct.com

**Easy Cookin'**
Cookware & cooking demonstrations
7121 Overland Road
Boise, ID 83709
877-392-6656
www.easycookin.com

**Epicurious**
Comprehensive website for recipes and culinary definitions
www.epicurious.com

**Ethnic Grocer**
Authentic foods from all over the world
Bensenville, IL
312-373-1777
www.ethnicgrocer.com

**Gourmet Mushrooms and Products**
Gourmet and organic mushrooms, growing kits
Graton, CA
800-789-9121
www.gmushrooms.com

**The Huckleberry People**
Huckleberry jams, syrups, & sauces
Missoula, MT
800-735-6462
www.huckleberrypeople.com

**Local Harvest**
Locate food sources by state
www.localharvest.org

**Lone Hawk Farm**
Elk steaks and sauage
Moscow, ID
www.lonehawkfarm.com

**Oakwood Game Farms**
Fresh & smoked gamebirds, wild rice
Princeton, MN
800-328-6647
www.oakwoodgamefarm.com

**Penzey's Spices**
Spices, herbs, and seasonings
800-741-7787
www.penzeys.com

**Prairie Harvest Specialty Foods**
Game meat, mushrooms, berries, foie gras
Spearfish, SD
800-350-7166
www.prairieharvest.com

**Snake River Farms**
Kobe beef and Kurobuta pork
Boise, ID
www.snakeriverfarms.com

**The Truffle Market**
Fresh truffles, mushrooms, gourmet items
Gettysburg, PA
800-822-4003
www.trufflemarket.com

**Valley Game & Gourmet**
Game meats, foie gras, patés plus recipes
Wholesale site: www.valleygame.com
Retail site: www.dinewild.com

# Glossary

*aioli* — A mayonaise base, strongly seasoned with garlic or other seasoning.

*al dente* — Italian for "to the tooth", describing pasta or other food cooked only until it offers a slight resistance when bitten into, but which is not soft or overdone.

*Asiago cheese* — A semifirm Italian cheese with a rich, nutty flavor, made from whole or part-skim cow's milk.

*bain-marie* — Similar to a double boiler, it is a 2-part container used to gently heat soups or sauces without allowing them to continue cooking. The food is placed in the top part, which sits on top of the lower part containing hot water.

*béarnaise sauce* — A classic French sauce made with vinegar, wine, tarragon, and shallots, reduced and finished with egg yolks and butter.

*blanch* — To plunge food (usually vegetables or fruits) into boiling water briefly, then into cold water to stop the cooking process.

*braise* — To brown food (usually meats or vegetables) first in fat, then cook, covered, in a small amount of liquid at low heat for a long time.

*brown sauce* — A sauce traditionally made of a rich meat stock.

*brunoise* — A mixture of vegetables that have been finely diced or shredded, then cooked slowly in butter.

*chiffonade* — Similar to julienne, the process of cutting lettuce, endive, or herbs into thin even strips.

*chinois* — A very fine mesh cone-shaped metal sieve used for pureeing or straining. Often a spoon or pestle is used to press the food through it.

*clarify* — The process of clearing a cloudy substance, such as in stocks or wines, or of melting butter until the foam rises and is skimmed off.

*confit* — A French word from a term meaning "to prepare", used for meat that has been cooked and preserved in its own fat.

*court-boullion* — A broth composed of vegetables and herbs that are cooked for about 30 minutes, cooled, and strained. Usually used to poach fish or vegetables. May also contain wine, vinegar, or citrus juice.

*crème frâiche* — A thick, velvety cream that is slightly tangy and can be boiled without curdling. Can be purchased in gourmet markets, or made at home by adding buttermilk to heavy cream.

*demi-glace* — A rich brown sauce (usually meat stock) combined with Madeira or sherry and slowly cooked until it's reduced by at least half, to a thick glaze.

*demi-sec* — In cooking, it refers to reducing by half; in wine, it refers to the level of sweetness.

*french, to* — To trim fat or bone from a cut of meat.

*fumet* — Literally meaning "aroma", it is a concentrated stock usually made from fish or mushrooms and added to a sauce.

*gremolata* — A garnish added to a cooked dish, such as osso buco, for a fresh accent. It usually consists of minced parsley, citrus zest, garlic, oil, and salt.

*jasmine rice* — A rice often used in Asian cuisine. It is similar to basmati rice in flavor and fragrance, but at a lower cost.

*julienne* — A method of cutting vegetables into thin strips, usually about 1 inch by 1⁄16 inch.

***Kaffir lime leaf*** Essential in many Thai soups and curries, it has an unmistakable and refreshing taste and aroma that can not really be substituted. The leaves are double and dark glossy green.

***kosher salt*** An additive-free coarse-grained salt.

***matcha*** A powdered tea made from a very high quality tea. It can be founded in Japanese and Asian markets.

***mirepoix; mirepois*** A mixture of diced carrots, onion, celery, and herbs that is sauteed in butter.

***mirin*** A sweet, rice wine used in cooking to sweeten meat or fish dishes.

***mise en place*** A French term meaning to have all the ingredients necessary for a dish and be ready to combine for cooking.

***Mourvèdre*** A red-wine grape that imparts a spicy, peppery taste to its wines. It is often used aas a component in other wines to improve color and structure.

***osso bucco*** Shanks, usually veal, braised slowly in wine, stock and vegetables. The term is sometimes used for dishes cooked the same way with other meats.

***paella*** A Spanish dish combining meats, shellfish, vegetables, and rice, and usually flavored with saffron.

***pancetta*** Slightly salty Italian bacon cured with salt and spices, but not smoked.

***panko*** Coarse Japanese bread crumbs used for coating fried foods.

***phyllo; filo*** Thin layers of pastry dough used in sweet and savory recipes.

***prosciutto*** Italian word for ham that is seasoned, salt-cured, air-dried, but not smoked.

***Prosecco*** A grape grown in the Veneto region of Italy and made into Prosecco wine. The wine is available as fully sparkling, lightly sparkling, and also still, has a crisp flavor with a taste of apple.

***purée*** To grind or mash food until it is completely smooth, using a food processor or blender, or by forcing the food through a sieve.

***quenelle*** A light dumpling made of minced or ground fish, meat, or vegetables, seasoned and bound with eggs. The mixture is formed into small ovals and gently poached in stock.

***roux*** A mixture of equal parts flour and butter used to thicken sauces. Cooking different lengths of time results in different flavors and colors.

***sambal oelek*** A condiment popular in Indonesia and southern India, it is usually made with chiles, brown sugar, and salt. It usually accompanies rice and curried dishes.

***sauté*** To quickly cook food over direct heat in a small amount of hot oil.

***sec*** French word for "dry".

***veloute*** A basic white sauce made with a white or light golden roux and veal, chicken, or fish stock.

***yuzu*** A sour citrus fruit from Japan. Its rind, or a powder made from the rind is used to brighten flavors. Sold in some Asian markets. The rind is very aromatic and very different from lemon or lime rind.

***zest*** The brightly colored outermost skin of citrus fruits, removed with a zester, grater, or paring knife.

# Index

## – D –



## – E –



## – F –

## –G–



## –H–



## –I–



## –J–



## –K–



## –L–

## – M –



## – N –



## – O –



## – P –



## – R –

## – S –

## – T –



## – V –



## – W